Corporate Governance

CORPORATE GOVERNANCE

History, Evolution and India Story

PRAVEEN B MALLA PHD

ROUTLEDGE
Routledge
Taylor & Francis Group
LONDON NEW YORK NEW DELHI

First published 2010
By Routledge
912–915 Tolstoy House, 15–17 Tolstoy Marg, New Delhi 110 001

Simultaneously published in UK
by Routledge
2 Park Square, Milton Park, Abingdon, Oxfordshire OX14 4RN

First issued in paperback 2015

Routledge is an imprint of the Taylor & Francis Group, an informa business

Typeset by
Bukprint India
B-180A Guru Nanak Pura, Laxmi Nagar,
Delhi 110 092

British Library Cataloging-in-Publication Data
A catalogue record of this book is available from the British Library

ISBN 13: 978–1–138–66274–2 (pbk)
ISBN 13: 978–0–415–58990–1 (hbk)

Dedicated to the memory of my

Late father

M.R. Rao

Contents

Preface

As a corporate governance researcher, I have always been on the lookout for a book that explains the concept in a very simple yet forceful way. For me, complicating simple ideas is a science and simplifying complex ideas, an art. And I prefer the latter.

This book is aimed at the novice student of corporate governance who wants to understand the basics of the concept. There are no pretensions about this book. Wherever needed, the language is allowed to lisp and at times I indulge in providing a flight to the readers' thoughts. I have written the book the way I would want to read it. I hope that the novice reader will not be let down. Some ideas are reiterated across chapters, deliberately. My agenda is very simple: the novice reader should have a fairly strong understanding of the concept by the time she completes reading the book.

Ever since the corporate form with limited liability emerged, the problems of corporate governance made their way into corporations. It is difficult to say precisely when this term was first coined. But both the academics and researchers concur that not before the year 1932 was corporate governance viewed seriously.

The recent proliferation in corporate governance literature has focused on ways that corporations work. The firm behavior was earlier modeled on the 'black-box' argument of the neo-classicists who asserted that firms are nothing more than production counters. All activities of the firm were so geared as to maximize profits. Finance literature has come a long way in explaining the various theories of firms and the behaviors associated with them. However, with the increasing awareness that mere economic and production-based explanations do not adequately describe the motivations for governance, researchers have focused on the behavioral side of the firm performance to justify the economic rationale of their typical behaviors.

Ronald Coase's seminal work in 1937 on the nature of the firms, where he emphasizes the importance of authority and direction that characterize the boundaries of the firm, has revolutionized the way researchers perceive firm behavior. His work gained further impetus with Alchian and Demsetz viewing the firm as a web of contractual relations. Monitoring team production could only be possible if the firm was characterized by contractual obligations. Subsequent development of agent-theoretic models, following Jensen and Meckling's seminal article "Theory of the firm: managerial behavior, agency costs and ownership structure", has focused on the behavioral motivations of individuals who run corporations.

However, the foundational argument of corporate governance as seen by the academic as well as other independent researchers can be traced back to the pioneering work of Berle and Means who observed, as early as in the 1930s, that the modern corporations having grown gigantically can separate the control over a firm from ownership. Erstwhile promoters who largely controlled and managed organizations, increasingly needed specialized skills. Professionals with the required skills were to be hired. Berle and Means' observation on the departure of the owners from the actual control of the corporations led to a renewed emphasis on the behavioral dimension of the theory of the firm.

The modern-day uproar over corporate governance problems—of insider trading, excessive executive compensation, managerial expropriation of shareholders' wealth, false reporting, accounting non-disclosures and self dealing, among others—are assumed to be related to the theory of separation of ownership and control.

Throughout the book, the connect to 'conflicts of interest' arising out of separation of ownership and control is constantly made through the different sections and chapters.

The importance and emergence of corporate governance in India is deeply influenced by the nature of relation that has existed between the corporate world on the one hand and the Indian state policies on the other. There are twin pressures exerting themselves on this relation. Between the post-Independence (post-1947) and pre-liberalization period, the 'relation' between the industry and the State was particularly susceptible to lack of accountability in terms of certain corporate governance norms. This period can be largely understood in terms of a relationship-based governance model prominently adopted in Japan and Germany. The structure of the relationship between the industry and the State did exist but it was rather flawed from the perspective of corporate governance norms.

In the post-liberalization period (post-1991), the onset of market openness brought its own set of challenges and opportunities. Though the State-industry relation has not completely abated, it appears that market-oriented governance models are able to provide important insights into the functioning of corporations. An understanding of corporate governance functioning in India thus requires incorporating insights from both the relationship-based and market-oriented models.

India is at the crossroads in terms of charting a new path of adopting a corporate governance model. It needs to take due cognizance of insights from both schools of thought and perhaps create a new balanced model for other emerging economies. Some readers may disagree with the thought that Indian corporate governance model is still at the crossroads. The recent Satyam scam has exposed the holes in the market-oriented model and historically, corporate mis-governance in India can be attributed to the existence of shades of relationship-based governance model. So none of the two predominant models can explain away the Indian context easily.

The last section closely examines and analyzes the events that have stymied the evolution of corporate governance in India, in contrast to most other studies that have dealt with the evolution of corporate governance as a post-liberalization, post-globalization phenomenon.

The relationship that existed between the industry and the State has been looked at in detail to explain my contention that corporate mis-governance has plagued Indian corporate sector right from the time of India's Independence. I argue from two different perspectives—systemic and relationship-based—to explain the reasons that created the space for corporate mis-governance. At the end, the arguments converge at a single underlying explanation: the nexus between the industry and the State has been largely responsible for the failure of the corporate governance system in the country. Readers may realize that some of the facts and figures in the India story are dated, but suffice it to say that such dated facts and figures have been deliberately used to expose the industry-State nexus. Though the latest facts and figures do not take away from the arguments, still they do not explain the nexus as strongly as the dated ones do. Since the section was designed to enlighten the reader with the evolution of the concept of corporate governance, I have taken the researcher's liberty in the use of such facts and figures.

The purpose of this book is not to discuss current and past scams. The Satyam scam happened while I was midway through my book. My well-wishers suggested that I factor in the scam while writing this book. But my concept for the book has been rather different than giving the novice readers cases on corporate scams. Such cases are best reserved for an advanced level reader and would probably be part of my next book, if I dare to write one.

Feedback from the readers to improve the book is eagerly solicited and would be highly appreciated.

Praveen B Malla

Acknowledgements

On the personal front, I would like to acknowledge the sacrifices made by my late father M. R. Rao for making me what I am today. As a researcher I would like to thank my academic guru, Professor Shishir K Jha from IIT Bombay.

I would like to thank the following individuals/publishing houses for granting me permission to use content from the papers that I had published in their journals:

1. Andrew Smith, Emerald Group Publishing Limited, for the following papers:
   a. Bhasa, M.P., 2004, Understanding the Governance Quadrilateral, *Corporate Governance: The International Journal of Business in Society*, Vol. IV, No. 4, pp. 7–15.
   b. Bhasa, M.P., 2004, Global Corporate Governance: Debates and Challenges, *Corporate Governance: The International Journal of Business in Society*, Vol. IV, No. 2, pp. 5–17.
2. Ms. Pratima Kapse, ICFAI University Press, Copyright Cell, for the following papers:
   a. Bhasa, M.P., 2004, From Managing Agency System to Naresh Chandra Committee Report on Corporate Governance, *ICFAI Journal of Corporate Governance*, Vol. III, No. 2, pp. 63–79.
   b. Bhasa, M.P., 2003, From Property Rights to Shareholder-Stakeholder Debate: A Brief Look into the Emergence of the Notion of Corporate Governance, *ICFAI Journal of Corporate Governance*, Vol. II, No. 2, pp. 88–99.
   c. Bhasa, M.P., 2006, A Peep into Corporate Governance, *ICFAI Journal of Management Research*, August, Vol. V, No. 9, pp. 59–66.

d. Bhasa, M.P., 2005, Ownership Structure and Firm Performance: A Review of Literature, *ICFAI Journal of Corporate Governance*, Vol. IV, No. 4, pp. 29–49.
e. Bhasa, M.P., 2005, Relationship-based Model of Corporate Governance: A Competing Governance Model, *ICFAI Journal of Corporate Governance*, Vol. IV, No. 2, pp. 47–54.
f. Bhasa, M.P., 2007, Is (IT) Governance manifested in Path-dependent Behavior of the Firm, *ICFAI Journal of Management Research,* Vol. VI, No. 1, pp. 91–97.

3. Mr. James McConvill, Sandstone Academic Press, for the following paper:
   a. Bhasa, M.P. and S.K. Jha, 2007, Corporate mis-governance in Post-Independence India: Examining the Government-Industry Nexus, *Corporate Governance Law Review,* Vol. III, No. 3.

Concerted efforts have been made to avoid any copyright violations. Wherever needed, permission has been sought from copyright owners. Adequate care has been taken in citing the right sources and references. However, should there be any errors or omissions, they are inadvertent and the author apologizes for the same. The author would be grateful should such errors be brought to his notice and assures that corrections would be incorporated in the future reprints or editions of this work.

For a working professional, writing a book can be a strenuous activity. It is a boon to have an editor who understands the demands of a full-time job and who sets realistic deadlines. I am grateful to Deepa Jagdish, my commissioning editor from Taylor and Francis, who has played a key role in getting me rolling and for nudging me to come out with this book.

List of Abbreviations

BIFR	Board of Industrial and Financial Reconstruction
BoD	Board of Directors
CALPERS	California Public Employees' Retirement System
CEO	Chief Executive Officer
CERC	Central Electricity Regulatory Commission
CG	Corporate Governance
CII	Confederation of Indian Industries
CSR	Corporate Social Responsibility
CSRC	China Securities Regulatory Commission
DFI	Development Financial Institution
DFID	Department for International Development
ESOP	Employee Stock Option Plan
ICICI	Industrial Credit and Investment Corporation of India
IDBI	Industrial Development Bank of India
IFCI	Industrial Finance Corporation of India
IMF	International Monetary Fund
IPO	Initial Public Offer
IRDA	Insurance Regulatory and Development Authority
KMBC	Kumar Mangalam Birla Committee
LIC	Life Insurance Corporation
MD	Managing Director
MIS	Management Information Systems
NFO	New Fund Offer
NGO	Non-Governmental Organization
NPA	Non-Performing Asset

OECD	Organization for Economic Co-operation and Development
PR	Public Relations
PSU	Public Sector Unit
SAIL	Steel Authority of India Limited
SEBI	Securities and Exchange Board of India
SEC	Securities and Exchange Commission
SHSE	Shanghai Stock Exchange
SICA	Sick Industrial Companies Act
TCS	Tata Consultancy Services
TISCO	Tata Iron and Steel Company
TRAI	Telecom Regulatory Authority of India

Part I
Introduction

Chapter 1

Corporation and Governance

Over the last decade and a half, corporate governance has become a central issue globally, *Why*? Modern-day business is beset with changing operating paradigms. With corporations growing larger and larger and the need for capital multiplying manifold, the need to enter foreign capital markets and access them for their capital requirements has given rise to new challenges in the governance of international business. The pre-transition era was justified by the need to protect domestic markets, but with corporations growing in gargantuan proportions, the need to open up domestic markets for the entry of foreign business became a necessity.

After the Second World War, when economies needed to be rebuilt the world over, increased cooperation amongst countries became indispensable for international movement of goods and services. Capital lying idle in some countries had to move out to lubricate the economies of other countries. This sowed the seeds for growing internationalization of business. Prior to this, protectionist regimes seldom allowed any foreign intruder into their national business scene. The growth of corporations that led to the demand for more and more capital, prodded the protectionist regimes to open up their economies and enable more foreign investment to flow into the domestic business. Control and command-based structures had to be done away with. Instead, a new form of governance structure, which was led by market-based economic systems primarily dominated by the private sector, had to be embraced. Now most governments the world over, are relinquishing State control over industry and the private sector is given incentives to accept the new challenges of globalization. This is evident from the transition efforts made by the East European and some Asian countries, including India, following the Russian reform process (perestroika) which was initiated by the change in leadership in the mid-1980s.[1]

Economies with efficient economic policies and stable political systems are a big draw amongst the investors. Countries that have opened themselves to world markets and that have good legal systems in place providing protection to investors, have attracted more capital in the process of globalization. As the demand for capital is growing in both the developed and the developing economies, the need for establishing good governance practices has gained momentum. Thus, corporate governance has become a pressing problem.

Despite the established checks and balances that protect shareholders, many a business has collapsed in the face of governance and investor confidence has been shattered. Some prominent scandals that have heated up the corporate governance discussion are Barings Bank, Enron, Adelphia, Tyco, and Parmalat. Closer home LIC-Mundhra scam as far back as in 1957, Home Trade, Ketan Parekh scandal, Securities Scam of 1992, C R Bhansali scam, debt default by Jindal Group, MESCO scam, or even as simple a governance let-down as Bombay Dyeing's failure to prevent 'creeping' acquisition of its shares by Arun Bajoria, have all lent voice against the growing corporate misdemeanors and a need to harness them.

Since this book's main purpose is to introduce you to the concept of corporate governance, it is imperative to take you through a chronological understanding of the subject. It is important to understand each of the words in *corporate governance* individually, and as we progress through the chapters, you will be exposed to a variety of terms that are woven around this concept.

CORPORATION

Origin of the Corporation

There are different versions of the exact period of the birth of the corporation. During the early Middle Age, corporations existed in the form of universities and ecclesiastical orders and were barred from making profits. While some authors believe that the early Middle Ages was the harbinger of the modern corporate form, others argue that since corporations during this period existed only to serve the society and also since economic motive that is so very ingrained in the corporation as we see today was absent, Middle Ages was certainly not the forerunner of today's corporate form.

Business history studies have been few and far between; that leaves us with scant literature to trace the exact origins of today's corporations. However, most business historians concur that not until the East India Company received a charter from Queen Elizabeth in 1600 AD to commence its trading business, was the real corporation born. Chartered corporations were semi- or quasi-governmental institutions that remained in business as long as they enjoyed the confidence of the crown. A charter was accorded to corporations by the crown with a specific purpose, especially that of bringing together individual investors in financing large-scale projects.

Prior to the formation of the East India Company, a few enterprising individuals engaged independently in trading. They would buy tea, raw silk and spices from India and sell them at a profit in their home countries. These individual traders owned their ships and deployed them in their trading business. But as business grew bigger and bigger, the need to raise more capital to shore up shipping vessels for transportation grew, necessitating individual traders to come together and form a syndicate.

A closer look at the operations of the East India Company suggests that it was truly the predecessor of the modern corporate form. It had its corporate headquarters in London at East India House which monitored its global operations in continents as diverse as Asia, Europe and North America. The Committee of Correspondence, the highest executive body within the company, headed by the Examiner of Correspondence was responsible for all the issues pertaining to policies and strategies. The day-to-day operations of the company were run by the Examiner's office along with the Corporate Secretary amongst other important functionaries.

Shareholders held quarterly meetings and one-fourth of the total number of directors were elected annually by them. Directors enjoyed a four-year term with the company and had the opportunity to rejoin the committee of directors after a one-year break.

Control was exercised by the head office at London over its territorial offices through the examination of the annual financial reports and intelligent analysis of such reports. The East India House put reporting structures and procedures in place and insisted on strict adherence to established norms. Thus in more ways than one, East India Company bears strong resemblance to today's advanced corporations. Hence, one is given to believe that the roots of the modern-day corporation lie in the incipience of the East India Company.

What is a Corporation?

Since this book focuses on corporate governance, it is important for one to understand the meaning of corporation. Throughout the book we will be discussing concepts related to the governance of corporations.

Not all forms of business organization are called corporations. Sole proprietorship, partnership and company are the best known and most widely discussed forms of businesses.

Sole Proprietorship

What comes to your mind when you see a beauty parlor, a small-sized eatery, a grocery shop or a medical shop? Most such small business ventures are funded and managed by individuals and hence the term 'sole proprietorship.'

You will observe that most businesses around you are sole proprietorships. Why? That is mainly because of the ease in obtaining a license and minimum capital requirement to set up such sole proprietorship businesses.

Sole proprietorship businesses exist as long as the business enjoys sustainable patronage and does not need huge funding requirements. Since the equity capital of this form of business is largely limited to the personal wealth of the proprietor, sole proprietorships usually tend to remain small in size.

The best thing about sole proprietorship is that business decisions can be taken at will and are subject to the business acumen of the proprietor. Nimbleness and speed are permanent features of this form of business. Should the proprietor wish to introduce a new product line or, say, serve a new market, she can do so in a jiffy. All business decisions are subject to the volition of the proprietor. There are no shareholders to convince.

Personal income and business income are one and the same in sole proprietorships. The biggest limitation of such a form of business is that it cannot grow beyond a certain point, unless the owner is enormously wealthy and is desirous of expanding his/her scope of operations.

Partnership: When two or more than two people come together to own and manage a business entity, it is called partnership. Each partner contributes towards the total capital of the business organization. Also, each partner may bring in a unique skill or expertise to the partnership firm.

Is there a decent-sized restaurant near your residence? Go and enquire whether it is a sole proprietorship or a partnership firm. If it is a partnership firm, probe further and find out which partner brought what to the table. Partner A could have met 80% of the capital requirements, Partner B could have provided for real estate and Partner C a wealth of expertise in running restaurant operations. There could be various other forms and levels of contribution to the partnership.

Unlike sole proprietorships, partnership firms are legal entities. To set up a partnership firm, a partnership deed that details out the capital contributions, shares, rights, duties and obligations of the partners has to be executed.[2] Partners, as specified by the executed deed, reap the rewards of the business and also assume any resultant liabilities.

Corporation: Most medium- and large-sized businesses are organized as corporations. General Electric, Microsoft, Oracle, IBM are all examples of large corporations. In India, Reliance Industries, Bharti Enterprises, Hero Group, Wipro, TCS are examples of large private sector corporations, while Oil and Natural Gas Corporation, Bharat Petroleum, SAIL are examples of large public sector corporations. Corporations are owned by a diverse group of owners more popularly known as shareholders.

Corporations can be of many types, namely, for-profit, not-for-profit, closely held, public companies. Closely held companies are those that are owned by a small group of investors who do not trade in the shares of the company. Usually, during the initial stages of incorporation, companies are funded by a handful of investors. These investors may either manage the company on their own or entrust the management to professional managers. The company is not listed in the stock market and hence does not invite retail participation. Since the closely held company has the backing of a few individual investors, social consciousness is far stronger than in any other form of business organization. Owners and employees are one big family and during hard times, owners find it difficult to lay off their employees. Market expectations of a closely held company are nil and hence business decisions are not dictated by myopic needs. Business decisions are taken based on the collective acumen of the investors. Most closely held companies grow big, make themselves attractive to external investing entities like institutional or retail investors and list themselves in stock exchanges to raise additional capital.

You must have heard of the term Initial Public Offer, more popularly known as IPO. Meet a stock broker or a sub-broker near your place. Ask him what an IPO means and discuss with him the merits and demerits of IPO.

Most widely known corporations today are public companies. Public companies are characterized by diverse ownership groups such as promoters, institutional investors, foreign shareholders, corporations, retail shareholders. Such companies are listed entities and their shares are traded in the stock markets. Ownership is easily transferable and shares keep changing hands with every trade. Public companies are always at the mercy of the markets and their value appreciates or depreciates based on the market sentiments on a given trading day. Investors have a limited exposure to risk but enjoy substantial benefits should the stock of the company rise. A major advantage of being a public company is that it has more working capital at its disposal than any other form of organization.

While in some cases public companies are managed by the main promoters, a majority of public companies are managed by professional managers who assume control of the day-to-day operations of the company. The whole argument of corporate governance lies in the owners' entrustment of the reins of the company to the professional managers. Owners/promoters and managers might not have similar interests and it is this "conflict of interests" that paves the way for corporate mis-governance. We will learn more about this concept in the chapters to come.

Definition of Corporation

The word corporation has its roots in the Latin word *corpus* which means a body of people. It is this collection of individuals that is responsible for giving direction and managing the operations of the corporation.

Corporation has been defined in many ways by many authors. However, its essence remains the same: it is a legal entity, is made of a collection of many individuals and has a distinct personality from those of its members.

The most common definition of corporation is "…. a legal, fictitious and moral entity, which has a legal personality distinct from those of its members."

Braendle et al define corporation as "… a person in its own right. The owners of the company are the shareholders (also called members). In return for money they put into the company, they are getting shares. Corporations are managed by directors, which [sic] may be members of the company or not."

Michael C. Jensen and William H. Meckling, the widely celebrated authors of the *Theory of the Firm*, in their paper "Corporate Governance and Economic Democracy: An Attack on Freedom" define the corporation as "a legal entity which serves as a nexus for a very complex set of contracts among human beings."

Perhaps the most comprehensive definition of corporation was given by Stewart Kyd, who authored the first treatise on corporate law in English. He defined corporation as

> a collection of many individuals united into one body, under a special denomination, having perpetual succession under an artificial form, and vested, by policy of law, with the capacity of acting, in several aspects, as an individual, particularly of taking and granting property, of contracting obligations, and of suing and being sued, of enjoying privileges and immunities in common, and of exercising a variety of political rights, more or less extensive, according to the design of its institution, or the powers conferred upon it, either at the time of creation, or at any subsequent period of its existence.

In the words of Melvin Eisenberg

> the business corporation is an instrument through which capital is assembled for the activities of producing and distributing goods and services and making investments. Accordingly, a basic premise of corporate law is that a business corporation should have as its objective the conduct of such activities with a view to enhancing the corporation's profit and the gains of the corporation's owners, that is, the shareholders.

Margaret Blair in her book *Ownership and Control: Rethinking Corporate Governance for the Twenty-First Century* defines corporations as "legal devices for assembling and organizing capital, labor and other resources to produce and sell goods and services."

In his article "The History of the Corporation", Lee Drutman has a slightly different take on the definition of the corporation. He looks at the corporation from the dependence perspective and says "Corporations stand as the most dominant institutions in our society. They provide the products and services upon which most of us have come to depend."

Corporation, thus, is a legal entity that is owned and financed by a diverse group of owners known as the shareholders, who enter into a contract with professional managers to run the day-to-day operations of the company. Together they strive to meet the demands of their stakeholders, be it providing products and services to the consuming public, meeting the operational norms set by the government and regulatory bodies, providing employment opportunities or fulfilling social commitments in societies they operate in.

Characteristics of a Corporation

There are a number of features that distinguish the corporation from any other form of business. Some of them are:

Legal Personality: A corporation has a distinct legal identity. It is recognized by law as a legal entity, separate from its owners/promoters and other shareholders. It can sue and be sued in its name. Also, it may own property, borrow or lend money, enter into contracts, own assets or incur liabilities and pay taxes.

Limited Liability: A corporation is owned by multiple shareholders and the liability of each shareholder is limited to the amount invested in the corporation by them. Creditors cannot claim from the personal wealth of shareholders. Should there be any liabilities, the shareholders bear no obligation once their portion of the share capital is paid up.

Easy Transferability of Ownership: Do you or your relatives own shares of any public company? Have you ever seen shareholders sell their shares in the stock market? What does this mean? One can transfer one's share of ownership rights to a buyer who is interested in buying the stock of the company. A corporation has no say in the trading of shares in the stock markets. It cannot restrain a seller from selling nor can it prevent a buyer from becoming a part owner of the corporation. A corporation can only play the role of a record keeper of its owners.

Management: Corporations are characterized by professional managers. In closely held companies, promoters usually double up as managers. In publicly held companies, investors entrust management to professional managers. These professional managers are responsible for running the day-to-day operations of the corporation.

Capital Acquisition: Corporations have the liberty to sell their stocks or bonds in the market to raise additional capital and fund projects that need additional investment. Easy transferability of ownership and limited liability come as a boon to corporations desirous of raising additional capital.

Unlimited Life: Corporations can acquire an immortal status provided they have the charter to conduct business. Death of investors and shareholders does not deter the corporation from continuing its operations. As long as it has the necessary capital to keep itself operational, the corporation lives on. In some cases, despite bankruptcy, corporations live on expecting bail-outs.

Multiple Stakeholders: Corporations live in societies and affect the day-to-day living of a multitude of stakeholders. Managers and employees who serve the corporation, collaboration partners or joint ventures that help it provide its services, suppliers who supply raw materials, customers who buy its products, investors who invest in its shares, creditors who provide debt capital, governments that legislate and facilitate its existence, communities and environment around which it exists and that are affected by its policies—all these are stakeholders of the corporation.

GOVERNANCE

We live in a heterogeneous society. Not all individuals are alike, nor do they think alike. Had all of us thought or behaved in a similar fashion, there would be no criminals in the society nor would there be any need for law-keepers. Growth in any sphere of life can be achieved only when there are different perspectives amonsgst the actors involved. Every individual is motivated by his/her own unique need. If every individual had his/her own way, society could witness lawlessness. To control and govern human behavior, certain rules are made mandatory in the society. While it would be convenient to surmise that rules would take care of any potential lawlessness, individuals belie such a hypothesis. To achieve personal gains, individuals can infringe on the general good of the society. Given the heterogeneity in individual perceptions, the available resources could be wasted with each individual trying to assert his/her supremacy over the other by channelizing the resources to his/her personal gain. It is to subordinate such individual interests to the general interest that governance is needed.

Corporations, if left unbridled, can hold the society to ransom. Remember, corporations have to exhibit their unquestioned loyalty to the shareholders first. Only then are the other stakeholders' interests considered. Assume that a manufacturing unit in order to save costs has decided not to invest in an effluent treatment plant. Instead it releases its effluents into the local sewage drains or the nearby river. What would happen to the communities living nearby? What would happen to the environment? While the shareholders' interests are served, the community at large is exploited. It is to control such value expropriation from stakeholders that governance is needed. Even in a case where the corporation is excessively concerned about the stakeholders and not concerned about its investors' interests, governance is required. The reason being, the value of one entity is being appropriated for the benefit of the others. Governance ensures an optimal and efficient mechanism by which each stakeholder gains optimally in value in such a way that no other stakeholder feels or experiences his/her value expropriation. Governance helps in exercising authority, giving direction and controlling a corporation so that its objective is achieved.

Of late there is a growing conviction that governance should not be left to the corporate boards alone. A certain amount of government and public involvement is necessary to drive the governance of corporations. Today, the financial institutions and other market participants along with the regulatory bodies and global legal requirements are exercising enormous influence on the governance systems of corporations.

What is Governance?

In its broadest sense, governance refers to the way in which a corporation or a nation is directed, controlled and run through the exercise of authority vested in the people governing them. Let us try to understand the concept of governance by first dwelling on a very popular governance type i.e., political governance. The same idea can be extrapolated to suit the other forms of governance as well, be it corporate governance or societal governance.

Political Governance: We are all aware that we elect political leadership through elections.[3] Have you ever asked yourself why we elect them in the first place? Political leaders are representatives of the people who have elected them. In a way, they represent the voice of a multitude of citizens. Imagine every citizen voicing his/her opinion and expecting the others to accept such opinions! Wouldn't there be too much of confusion with myriad opinions to choose from? Political governance is the process of decision-making by a select group of people, elected by the citizens. It refers to the way in which governments interact with the citizens, external governments, institutions and other agencies in formulating, evaluating and implementing legislations. Political governance entails the entire gamut of setting up of processes right from legislating to implementing; from influencing the country's economic and social development to monitoring the behavior of institutions, corporations and other agencies; from facilitating growth for individual citizens to building administrative mechanisms to meet the needs of the society; and from controlling crime to providing mechanisms for dispute resolution. Given the sheer diversity that governments operate in, governance can be a very tough proposition.[4] Good governance not only leads the country to economic growth but also helps in maintaining social balance and keeps the citizens happy.

Corporate Governance: As we have understood from the previous sections, a group of diverse investors own the corporation. These investors, popularly known as shareholders, entrust the management of the corporation to professional managers. The professional managers may not share the same objectives as those of the shareholders. They could take business decisions influenced by their personal interests. Such a thing can be detrimental to the general well-being of the corporation. Hence, businesses are monitored by boards that have either the shareholders or their representatives as directors. The board of directors has a fiduciary responsibility towards the larger stakeholder community. They are responsible for articulating the vision of the corporation, setting up teams to monitor its performance, controlling deviant managers and looking after the general well-being of all their stakeholders.

Good corporate governance immunizes corporations from failures, financial distress and stakeholder value expropriation. Corporate governance is a mechanism by which shareholders are assured of their returns, creditors are assured of their payments, business stakeholders are assured of the business' continuity, and society's social and environmental needs are taken care of.

Good corporate governance ensures efficient allocation of a firm's resources and assets, attracts low-cost capital thereby reducing the overall costs of producing goods and services, and meets the expectations of all the stakeholders that the firm impacts.

According to an OECD report of 1998, good corporate governance follows the principles of fairness, transparency, accountability and responsibility[5]—fairness in protecting shareholder rights and ensuring enforceability of contracts with resource providers; transparency in timely disclosures on corporate financial performance, governance and ownership-related issues; accountability in terms of clarifying roles and responsibilities of the executives and the board oversight of management; and responsibility in complying with legislations.

Definition of Corporate Governance

There is no single definition for the term "corporate governance". Different authors have defined corporate governance in different ways. While institutions and committee reports have defined corporate governance very broadly, finance researchers have advanced definitions that focus excessively on the financial return on investments. Stakeholder theorists, on the other hand, have tried to provide definitions that not only talk of maximizing returns to shareholders but also to other stakeholders. Some authors have looked at corporate governance from a contract or a behavioral or relationship/network perspective and hence define it accordingly.

Below are listed a representative sample of such definitions.

Broader and neutral definitions

Corporate governance is the system by which companies are directed and controlled. Boards of directors are responsible for the governance of their companies. The shareholders' role in governance is to appoint the directors and the auditors, and to satisfy themselves that an appropriate governance structure is in place.

The Cadbury Report, 1992, Para 2.5

Corporate governance is the relationship between various participants in determining the direction and performance of corporations.

Monks and Minow

Corporate governance defines a set of relationships between a company's management, its boards, its shareholders and other stakeholders.

OECD Principles of Corporate Governance, 2004

Corporate governance can be defined as the mechanisms transmitting signals from product markets and input markets into firm behavior.

Berglof and von Thadden

One of the most comprehensive broader definitions has been provided by Charles Oman in his technical paper produced as part of the OECD's research programme on Corporate Governance in Developing Countries and Emerging Economies.

Defined broadly,

> corporate governance refers to the private and public institutions, including laws, regulations and accepted business practices, which together govern the relationship, in a market economy, between corporate managers and entrepreneurs ("corporate insiders") on one hand, and those who invest resources in corporations, on the other. Investors can include suppliers of equity finance (shareholders), suppliers of debt finance (creditors), suppliers of relatively firm-specific human capital (employees) and suppliers of other tangible and intangible assets that corporations may use to operate and grow.

Definitions that advocate governance in the interests of the shareholders

Corporate governance describes ways of ensuring the corporate actions, assets and agents are directed at achieving the corporate objectives established by the corporation's shareholders.

Sternberg

Corporate governance is a field of economics that investigates how corporations can be made more efficient by the use of institutional structures such as contracts, organizational designs and legislation. This is often limited to the question of shareholder value i.e., how the corporate owners can motivate and/or secure that the corporate managers will deliver a competitive rate of return.

Henrik Mathiesen

Amongst the most popular of modern day definitions of corporate governance is the one given by Shleifer and Vishny in their paper "A survey of corporate governance" where they include other ownership groups in addition to the shareholders. However, the focus is still on the investors. "Corporate governance deals with the ways in which suppliers of finance to corporations assure themselves of getting a return on their investment."

All these definitions point to the role of actors central to corporate governance, who are involved in 'working out means' to obtain returns for some investment that they have made.

Definitions that advocate the interests of stakeholders, including shareholders

Corporate governance refers to the design of institutions to make managers internalize the welfare of stakeholders in the firm.

Tirole

Corporate governance is more than simply the relationship between the firm and its capital providers. Corporate governance also relates to how the various constituencies that define the business enterprise serve, and are served by, the firm. Explicit as well as implicit relationships between the corporation and its employees, customers, creditors, suppliers and host communities (and the dynamics of the relationships among these constituencies) fall within the boundary of an embracing definition of corporate governance.

Tony Naughton

Definitions that look at corporate governance outside the shareholder-stakeholder window

It is an entire network of formal and informal relations involving the corporate sector and society in general.

Keasey and Wright

It is a complex set of constraints that shape the ex-post bargaining over the quasi-rents generated by a firm.

Zingales

The behavior of individuals within the firms is thus central to understanding the current day corporate governance.

Thus one can simply define corporate governance as a mechanism by which people governing the corporations ensure that benefits accrued to all the stakeholders are so optimized that the value of no one single stakeholder is ameliorated to the detriment of the others.

Is Governance the same as Management?

During the course of your management studies you would have come across the terms "governance" and "management" quite frequently. In many cases, both the terms have been used interchangeably. But is governance the same as management? About a century ago, governance could pass off as management and vice versa. *Why*? Businesses were owned and managed by promoters and hence their actions always had to support their vision. As businesses started growing larger and larger, more and more capital was needed and the number of owners gradually increased.

Professionals had to be brought in to run the operations of the corporation because (a) multiple owners had their own interests in contributing to the corporation and hence conflicts of interest could arise; and (b) promoters lacked the skill and expertise demanded by modern-day corporations.

Way back in the 1930s, Columbia University professors Adolph A Berle and Gardiner C Means observed that separation of ownership and control had slowly seeped into the business psyche. This separation in itself later became the source of corporate mis-governance. We will deal with this concept in the chapters to come.

Governance thus got delineated from management, post the 'separation of ownership and control' scenario. While governance remained with the owners/promoters, management went to the professionals.

To put simply, management is defined as doing things right. It is an organizational function that deals with the entire operational spectrum right from planning to controlling business operations. It derives its power and authority from governance. Good management is that which delivers on the organizational mission, on time and within budgets.

Governance, on the other hand, plays the role of the enabler. It provides for policies and procedures that help management to do things right. Governance plays a major role in protecting the interests of the corporation's stakeholders. It not only endeavors to align the management's interests with its own interests but also plays a monitoring role by keeping a keen watch on the management's performance. It is incumbent upon governance to meet the requirements of accountability, transparency and ethical business conduct.

SUMMARY

This chapter has laid the foundation for the chapters to come in this book. It has dealt with the meanings of corporation and governance, separately. While the origin of the corporation throws light on the historicity of governance, the chapter wades through the multiple variants in which governance has been defined. Different perspectives on corporate governance drive home the point that the term/concept is not as simple as it may look. Every stakeholder understands corporate governance from his or her prism and thus that makes it a very complicated science. The chapter has also laid down the need for governance and explicated the difference between management and governance. We have also realized that the demand for foreign capital has driven the need for corporate governance. In the next chapter, we will try and understand the evolution of the concept of corporate governance from a theoretical perspective.

DISCUSSION QUESTIONS

1. Refer to the scams mentioned in the chapter. Pick two scams that interest you. Ask your friends to choose a couple of them. Search the internet for more information on the chosen scams. Discuss amongst yourselves what you think caused such scams?
2. What is the difference between a sole proprietorship and a corporation? Explain with examples.
3. Define corporation. What are the characteristics of a corporation?
4. Explain governance within the context of political governance and extend the notion to corporate governance.
5. Are governance and management one and the same? Explain with examples.

NOTES

1. Crama, Y. et al (1997), "Corporate Governance Structures, Control and Performance in European Markets: A Tale of Two Systems", Working Paper, Tilburg—Centre for Economic Research. Djankov, S. (1999), "Ownership Structure and Enterprise Restructuring in Six Newly Independent States", Working Paper, World Bank. Also see Estrin, S. et al (2001), "The Effect of Ownership and Competitive Pressures on Firm Performance in Transition Countries: Micro-evidence from Bulgaria, Romania and Poland", Working Paper, Licos Centre for Transition Economies.
2. Chandra, P., (2007), *Financial Management*, 7th Edition, pp. 11.
3. Let us assume that we live in a sane nation and not under a dictatorial regime. Even in the case of a dictatorial regime, the explanation that follows holds good.
4. All governments, by their very definition, govern. The result can either be good governance or bad governance.
5. Business Sector Advisory Group, Report to the OECD on Corporate Governance: Improving Competitiveness and Access to Capital in Global Markets at 20, (April 1998), (the "Millstein Report").

Chapter 2

CORPORATE GOVERNANCE: THEORETICAL FOUNDATION

In the previous chapter we understood what corporate governance means. We have also understood its need and importance. But as mentioned in Chapter 1, is corporate governance a recent phenomenon? The answer to this is both yes and no. Corporate governance as a business best practice was prevalent right from the day the modern form of corporation emerged. Yet it was the Enron debacle and other corporate scandals that have led to the growth of the concept of corporate governance. Today, corporate governance is considered more seriously than ever before because of the growth in the type and number of stakeholders and their ever growing expectations from the corporations.

The theory of separation of ownership and control propounded by Adolph A. Berle and Gardiner C. Means[1] lay the foundation for generations of research in understanding the nuances of corporate governance. Though most of the early literature concentrated on the expropriation of the shareholders' wealth by the managers, today corporate governance research has come of age and its scope has broadened.

A focused view of corporate governance issues can be established by questioning who is benefited and who should be benefited from corporate decisions or senior management actions.[2] A corporate governance issue exists when there is a conflict between "what is" and "what ought to be".

Conflicts arise whenever there are differences in perspectives amongst the actors involved. And wherever there are conflicts, problems of governance exist. The primary reason for conflicts in interest amongst the actors in a firm is their differing objectives. Though many theories of firm have been propounded over the past few decades, it is seen that not many authors have focused on the behavioral aspects of a firm. The theory of markets passed off as the theory of firms. Economic theories have taken a long time to explain the rationale for the existence of the firms and have severely failed to explain the boundaries and internal organization of firms. All that the economists proffered as the theory of firms was subsumed in the basic argument of "price theory".

For long, economists were of the view that the analysis of the internal working of the firms was not their job. Instead, they explained the functioning of the economy with markets as their explananda. For them firms were mere actors in the markets. The neo-classicists viewed the firm as a "black-box" whose only function was to maximize profits or maximize present value by meeting the relevant marginal conditions with respect to inputs and outputs.

However, the pioneering work of Coase and later, the work of Alchian and Demsetz have stimulated research on the "theory of firm". The nature of firms began to be understood more vividly first in the arguments of property rights and then through arguments made by the agency-costs theorists. What is interesting to note is that though Berle and Means have observed a managerial revolution as early as the 1930s, it was not until Jensen and Meckling published a seminal article titled "Theory of the Firm: Managerial Behavior, Agency Costs and Ownership Structure" in 1976 that the implications of Berle and Means' firms[3] was openly acknowledged.

Literature in corporate governance is replete with empirical studies on the theory of separation of ownership and control. Major attempts have been made by researchers to build on or to justify the claims of the conflicts of interest theory. Berle and Means firms were taken as the starting point of any empirical dissection. Most studies have assumed widely diffused ownership structures and reams have been written on the "managerialist" literature focusing on the objectives/ intentions of managers under whose control corporations lay. The image of the widely held corporation has been central to the understanding of many nuances of corporate governance. However, the empirical validity of such an image is questionable. Some major research studies have shown that even amongst the largest of the American publicly traded firms, ownership concentration could be found and that the widely held firm is a rare phenomenon.[4] La Porta et al[5] have studied 27 wealthy economies across the world to identify the controlling shareholders. Their findings suggest that ownership is largely concentrated in most countries. They claim that ownership is not diffuse in countries where the legal framework to protect the interests of the dispersed shareholders is weak. Original owners in such countries are compelled to own large blocks of shares and align their incentives with other shareholders.

The whole notion of corporate governance hinged on the "rights" of actors involved in the operations of the firm as well as the "costs" involved to protect these rights of the actors. Property rights and agency costs theories were the precursors of the corporate governance theory of separation of ownership and control, in a way. These theories went a long way in explaining how resources are allocated; the incentives involved in proper allocation of resources; the emergence of a new breed of agents who took care of the principal owners' property; the differing objectives of these agents; the incentives needed to be given to the agents to align their interests with the owners' interests, and the types of costs incurred by the principal to avoid conflicts of interest.

Different theories of firms employed different explananda to understand the way firms behave. While some have emphasized on the contractarian arguments, others have exclusively looked at communitarian dimensions to explain firm behavior. In this chapter, we make an attempt at understanding the evolution of the concept of corporate governance through the prism of firm behavior. We begin with understanding property rights theory which is considered the first forerunner of today's corporate governance debate. Going further, we try and understand the human element in the firm behavior through two theories—nexus of contracts and agency theory. Following these theories, you will understand how corporate governance in popular parlance has come about being associated with diversely held corporations, more conventionally called the Berle and Means firms. The evolution discussion would culminate with the stakeholder debate which is the most modern way of understanding what corporate governance means.

Property Rights Theory

Property is a resource on which we assume and assert to have a right by virtue of our ownorship. Different disciplines have treated the concept of property differently. However, all theories concur that property does not refer to the relationship between individuals and things but between individuals with regards to things. There are different types of property: movable, immovable, public, private, and intellectual, to name a few. Definitions of each of the property types are not within the scope of this book. Our focus is to understand corporate governance from the prism of property rights.

Property rights essentially mean the ability to enjoy a piece of property by individuals who own them. Economic property rights are the rights an individual has over a commodity or an asset, which he/she through his/her ability, can consume either directly or indirectly through exchange. Legal property rights, on the other hand, are rights that are recognized in part or whole and are enforced by the government. Legal property rights arise when others expropriate the property of an individual and the individual is left defenseless to stop this appropriation.

The economic rights that individuals have over their assets are never absolute. Property rights are a function of the attempts made by an individual to maximize his/her gains from the assets; the protection that he/she can afford to give to his/her assets from expropriation by other individuals; the depreciation value of the assets over time; the anachronistic attribute of the assets and also the legal setting in which the owner owns the assets. The value of the property could depreciate if adequate efforts are not made by the owner to maximize its entire potential. However, it should be understood that the owner with his/her limited resources and/or limited knowledge of the attributes of the assets that he/she possesses, might not be in a position to bring in material changes to the growth in the assets. Individuals who specialize in understanding the attributes of those assets are to be roped in if the owner has to make potential gains from the assets.

Where individuals other than the owner are involved in realizing the potential gains of the assets, the problem of delineation of rights arises. The onus of protecting his/her assets from being appropriated by individuals employed by him/her lies with the owner. The non-owners may through their actions depreciate the value of the assets without actually fully bearing the costs of their actions. To contain this uncompensated exploitation and to realize the maximization of the net value of the assets, a distinct form of ownership or ownership pattern must emerge.

To specify his/her individual rights, the owner may determine how the costs and rewards would be allocated among the individuals in the organization for efficient utilization of the resources and thereby for maximizing gains on the assets employed. Individual rights can be specified only through contracts, either implicit or explicit. The nature of the contracts would thus play a vital role in the behavior of the individuals involved in executing the owners' assets for potential gains. However, the importance of ownership cannot be discounted since it is the only available mechanism through which rights are conferred upon the owner to make decisions in all contingencies that are not specified in the initial contract.

Property rights literature thus has laid a very strong foundation to the understanding of the theory of the firm and hence corporate governance.

Nexus of Contracts

What does the electorate do when it casts its vote in favor of a political candidate in elections? It enters into an unsaid contract with the candidate where it promises to vote in return for fulfillment of its privately defined objectives, which is otherwise not possible in simple social exchanges. What if the elected candidate refuses to honor his/her electorate?

What do you do when you pay for your ticket in a public bus? You enter into an unsaid contract with the transporter for a ride. What if the transporter fails to drop you at the destination for which the fare has been collected?

Likewise, what does a corporation do when it establishes itself in the society? It enters into an unsaid contract to take care of the needs of the society by providing employment, products and services, and also guarantees socially responsible behavior. What if the corporation refuses to provide acceptable level of goods and services? What if it releases its toxic effluents into your city's river?

In all the three examples above, you would cry hoarse about the breach in contract. But how often do you take action on injustice meted out to you? As individuals, it is difficult for us to precisely comprehend the unsaid contract and take action. *Why*?

Just imagine what would happen to the firm if there were no written contract. A firm, as you are by now aware, interacts not only with its shareholders, but also with its suppliers and vendors, customers, employees, government, communities and many other stakeholders. A firm's existence and relationship with its stakeholders is governed by contracts. So, the firm is a nexus of contracts. It tries to balance the conflicting objectives of the various stakeholders through contractual obligations.

Viewing the firm as a set of contractual relationships among individuals with conflicting interests, requires us to look into the nature of the contracts and the agreement on the contracts arrived at by the individuals.

Anticipating all possible future contingencies to write a complete contract is impossible. Practically, writing a complete contract is difficult. Ex-ante forecasts of ex-post outcomes are a difficult task since behaviors of individuals cannot be predicted with accuracy. Moreover anticipating all future contingencies is not possible since firms do not exist in isolation. External factors like industry behavior, political and environmental conditions, behavior of markets that are subject to unprovoked fluctuations etc., affect the operations of the firms. In the light of the external disturbances, it is difficult to accurately foresee how individuals would react to future contingencies, and thus accommodating for conflicting contingent behaviors while writing a contract, is not an easy thing. Hence, complete contracts are too idealistic in nature and are conspicuously absent from all contractual agreements.

You have by now understood that writing an ex-ante contract factoring in all the future contingencies is impossible. So decisions are to be made ex-post both in terms of allocation of resources at contingent levels and also on the allocation of quasi-rents. Thus, there exists a scope for ex-post governance. The surfacing of the "incomplete contracts"[6] paradigm has thus helped the evolution of the theory of governance. Incomplete contracts contain in them the seeds of conflicts.[7] Costs are to be incurred if these conflicts are to be avoided. Agency theory literature has grown on this notion of "conflicts of interest" and the costs attached to these conflicts.

Agency Theory

Have you ever delegated your job to your friends, family members or associates? Have you ever asked your little sister to buy groceries for the month? Has your spouse ever delegated the job of responding to his/her business calls when he/she is away from home? In our daily life we often delegate or are delegated work. In business parlance, the delegate acts as the agent of the delegator who is the principal. How often do you think the delegate mirrors the principal's decisions while acting on his/her behalf?

To cite an example, you have asked your little sister to take charge of the month's grocery purchases. Your sister is now in a position to take a decision on which items to buy and which not to buy. For quite sometime now, she had been planning to buy a college backpack. This job has now come as a boon and she adds the backpack to her purchase. Also, she feels that it has been a long time since you bought those canned Bengali sweets. She uses her discretion in throwing in two such cans into her basket. A bottle of coke does not hurt anybody. She adds a bottle in her final purchase. She may be able to convince you by justifying her purchases. But the question is, were the principal's and the agent's interests aligned? Would you (principal) have bought the three unplanned items had you been in charge of groceries? Probably not! Why? Because your interests are possibly different from that of your sister's. Your sister being your agent should have mirrored your interests. But she hasn't. This is commonly known as "conflicts of interest" in business literature.

In this subsection, we thus set about understanding the principal-agent related issues, more popularly known as agency theory.

Agency theory has grown quite independent of the property rights theory. Both the theories are complementary to each other. The earliest proponents of the theory have been Stephen Ross[8] and Jensen and Meckling. Agency theory begins with the assumption that the agents through their conflicting objectives frustrate the attempts of the principals in maximizing gains over their assets. This leads to the development of asymmetries in the gains from the reciprocity of exchanges. The agency theory has led to the development of the standard principal-agent model.

The principal-agent model assumes that the agents would act opportunistically to further their personal objectives and hence their interests are put before the interests of the principal. By virtue of possessing more knowledge than the principals in the execution of resources, coupled with the guarantees provided by incomplete contracts, the agents are well positioned to create information asymmetries and may rob the principals of the value due to them. As Foss rightly puts it, agency theory is a model where the informed party trades with the uninformed party and where the private information in question may either concern what the agent does or what his/her characteristics are (Foss, 1997). The basic conclusion of the agency theory is that firm value cannot be maximized since managers possess discretion, which allow them to expropriate value to themselves (Turnbull, 2000).[9]

Drawing from the contracts argument in the previous subsection, it is difficult to propose a first-best contract given the diverse interests of the principals and agents. The hidden actions and hidden knowledge of the agent through which he/she can create information asymmetries cannot be assumed ex-ante and hence the principal-agent model comes within the ambit of governance.

Jensen and Meckling were the first to propose agency costs, which, they convincingly assert, will take care of the incentive conflicts. Assuming that both the agent and the principal are motivated to maximize their utility from the asset or resource, there is good reason to believe that there will be a divergence in their interests. The principal can, however, limit the divergence of the agent by incurring some monitoring costs. Monitoring costs refer to the costs incurred by the principal to check the aberrant behavior of the agent. These costs are "control costs", which are incurred in the efforts made by the principal to decide on the compensation policies, to set out budgets, to punish erring behavior of the agent, to audit the financial reports, etc.

Monitoring costs may not, however, completely eliminate the problems of incentive conflicts. Hence, bonding costs are incurred by the principal to ensure that all the decisions taken by the managers/agents are conducive to maximizing the gains of the principal. Bonding costs help in aligning the interests of the agent with the interests and objectives of the principal. Apart from the afore-mentioned costs, costs in the form of "residual loss" are also incurred by the principal. Residual loss refers to the quantum of loss or reduction in gains realized by the principal due to the divergence of the agents' interests. Residual loss occurs when monitoring costs incurred by the principal and the bonding costs expended by the agent are not effective enough to contain the conflicts in interest between the principal and the agents.

> *Inferring from the grocery example above, you have to incur all these costs to keep your little sister aligned to your interests. You could be incurring monitoring costs by making periodic calls on her mobile phone while she is shopping; bonding costs by allowing her to buy her backpack; and residual loss in the form of cost for the bottle of coke that she has added inadvertently to her purchase.*

Universally, in all situations that involve cooperative effort (and where one party has the resources and the other party the skill to deploy those resources in gainful activities), agency problems arise and agency costs need to be incurred. The need to induce the agent to indulge in maximizing the principal's utility value is general. Principal-agent problems are complex in cases where the principals are multiple in number than in cases where the principal is a single owner. A single owner supposedly has more powers than multiple or fractionated ownership to harness the agent. Also, the agency costs incurred by fractionated owners has to be much larger. Berle and Means have studied the ownership structures of American corporations in the early twentieth century and observed that a managerial revolution was in the offing with so many widely diffused firms. This they referred to as the classic case of "separation of ownership and control".

Berle and Means Firms

Why does your spouse hire a chauffeur to drive his/her car? Maybe because he/she is tired of the growing traffic and finds it difficult to maneuver on busy roads. Or maybe he/she wants to leave the job to a professional who he/she thinks can do the job much better than him/her. Or maybe he/she wants to utilize his/her time in some other activity while commuting. Or maybe he/she wants to enjoy the ride by looking out of the window. There could be multiple reasons for giving away the driver's seat to somebody else. In corporate governance literature, this is a typical example of separation of ownership and control. Your spouse is the owner of the car but the control is with the driver. This separation could be a potential cause for conflict of interests. While your spouse might want to shorten his/her commute time by taking the shortest route possible, the driver may take the longer route citing traffic jams on the shorter route. The driver may misuse the car for his personal purpose which is against your spouse's interests. Your spouse could be driving the driver nuts by constantly nagging him on his lack of driving skills and hence he rams the car into a tree. Instances mentioned here, if applied in the corporate world, constitute problems related to corporate governance.

This section helps you understand the concept of separation and control more clearly.

Corporate governance has in one form or the other existed in business since the birth of the limited liability form of the corporation. However, it was the pioneering work of Berle and Means that led to the development of an entire body of literature which focused on managerial expropriation of shareholder value. Different authors have studied corporate governance in different ways, yet the primary contribution has been to the body of knowledge which has its genesis in the Berle and Means theory of separation of ownership and control.[10] As early as in the 1930s, Berle and Means argued that corporations had acquired the attributes of powerful social institutions. They recognized that the modern corporations had become forces to reckon with and were unlike their predecessors which had their roots in a production-based system. The market-led economy has shaped the modern corporation into colossal giants. The wealth pool of corporations started growing with the advent of stock exchanges. Ordinary shareholders who had a passing interest in the corporation invested in them to make some quick gains. This led to the emergence of a new class of professionals (managers, whom the agency theory refers to as the agents) who took up the reins of the corporations in their hands.

Berle and Means' firms emerged to keep up with the demands of the technological and financial developments associated with large firms. Some researchers opine that such firms also arise when the legal system of a country provides adequate protection to the minority shareholders.[11] Since American firms were subject to lesser economic-based social conflicts than elsewhere, shareholders or the principals could afford to distance themselves from the operational activities of the firm without fearing that the managers would be captured by the social democratic pressures.[12]

The Berle and Means firms have to control agency costs if they are to prosper and survive. Though the benefits associated with such firms in the form of agglomeration of capital and the spread of risk cannot be discounted, the underpinnings of such firms in welfare societies is huge considering the fact that the mangers are in a better position to create information asymmetries, which, in turn helps them to expropriate shareholder value. In a diffusely held firm, no one shareholder is amply motivated to take the deviant managers head-on since the gains accrued from the deadlock would be marginal given the costs incurred to monitor any aberrant behavior by the managers.[13]

Separation of ownership from control thus led to the evolution of a market–based control mechanism. Shareholders who are dissatisfied with the performance of their agents can turn to the market to wash off their hands from the control they previously had on the corporation. The market thus dominates the governance process where control can be exchanged in lieu of "opting out" of the corporation's ownership by the existing shareholders.

This kind of an agent-led or owner-separated corporation setting is a highly efficient mechanism to the decision-making problems faced by large corporations.[14] Although the widely diffused firms emerged as efficient allocators of resources and hence became utility maximizers, the attendant risks of separation of ownership from control has brought to the fore the behavioral dimension of the agents' motivation in running the corporations. The excessive focus of the shareholders on pecuniary results coupled with the market-led forces like the existence of managerial labor markets, hostile takeovers, contests for corporate control etc., to contain managerial excesses, have compelled the managers to turn to short-term result-oriented performance. In the process of maximizing short-term benefits, the stakeholders of the corporations are conveniently forgotten.

The modern-day ruckus of insider trading, excessive executive compensation, managerial expropriation of shareholders' wealth, false reporting, non-disclosure of certain accounting and governance practices, self-dealing, and such other practices—all of which are intrinsic to current corporate governance problems, are assumed to be related to the theory of separation of ownership and control.

Shareholder–Stakeholder Debate

Though shareholders are yet to get their due in this era of managerial capitalism, another new generation of thought process has arisen which demands that the benefits of the corporation be maximized and extended to all those who are either directly or indirectly connected with it.[15] What was proposed as corporate social responsibility by Howard Bowen in the early 1950s gained impetus with academicians proposing a rehashed version of it with broader connotations and termed it the stakeholder theory.[16]

Over the last two decades, debates on corporate governance have focused on the contractarian view of business than on the communitarian dimension. Contractarian view refers to the primary importance being given to the shareholders since they are the ones who contract with the agents to run the corporations. Communitarian view, on the other hand, refers to the importance given to the stakeholders who are crucial to the corporation's existence. However, a spate of scandals and corporate misdeeds which have appropriated the community's value has led to the emergence of the stakeholder theory of business as a main challenger to the shareholder theory. Also, the stakeholder theory is considered to be an offshoot of political compulsions as against the shareholder theory.

The proponents of the shareholder theory argue that the shareholders are the principals in whose interest the corporations are run. Since they bear the residual risks,[17] agents should so act that the value of the shareholders are maximized as incentives for risk-bearing and waiting. Had the shareholders not invested in corporations and borne the attendant risks of depreciation of their value, society could not have enjoyed the benefits of the corporations' economic functions. Hence advocates of shareholder theory vehemently propose the primacy of shareholder value maximization. This excessive focus on the maximization of shareholder wealth has led to managerial myopia.[18]

In the modern finance literature, the shareholder theory of governance has received much support from the arguments posited by Milton Friedman who contends that business should not feel obligated to society explicitly, since the main function of business is to serve itself and while serving its purpose, business indirectly serves the interests of the society.[19] Lured by the prospects of maximizing shareholder wealth, managers adopt deviant methods to the detriment of the parties that have either direct or indirect stakes in the corporation. This led to the development of the stakeholder theory of corporate governance.

As O'Sullivan in her book *Contests for Corporate Control: Corporate Governance and Economic Performance in the United States and Germany* aptly puts it, stakeholder theory emerged as a rational response to the shareholder theory. The basic argument of stakeholder theory stems from the fact that the physical assets in which individuals invest are not the only assets that create value in the corporation. Shareholders are not the exclusive resource contributors, as the firm's decisions involve consequences for all stakeholders. Human assets, in which the individuals invest implicitly, create much more value than what can be estimated in economic terms.[20] Also, apart from the firm-specific human assets, society too bears a large part of the risk in terms of depletion of its resources, exploitation of its social capital, the excesses the environment encounters due to emission of toxic gases and waste products, involvement and the risk borne by the creditors who supply the needed capital over and above the equity capital, the efforts put by the suppliers to ensure the smooth running of the corporation, the tab that the future generations pick up as a result of the depletion of the society's asset base, etc. Hence all the parties who are either directly or indirectly affected by the corporation's operations are to be compensated either in monetary or non-monetary terms. This line of thought led to the argument that corporations must attempt to maximize stakeholders' interests instead of plainly focusing on shareholders' benefits.

Stakeholder theory is a modern evolution in keeping with the current-day business dynamics. Where shareholder theory dealt with only a diverse set of owner groups, stakeholder theory has emerged as a gigantic model with shareholders being considered as one amongst the many stakeholders affected by the performance of the firm. The scope of stakeholder theory has multiplied manifold. However, the basic tenet underlying the theory is the maximization of human welfare (and also the welfare of all living species), in whichever form it might be.

SUMMARY

This chapter has detailed the theoretical evolution of corporate governance. The whole concept of corporate governance has been looked at from the prism of "conflicts of interest", and theories governing such conflicts have been identified to delineate the nuances of today's corporate governance. The concept of property rights has been reckoned as the first theory to explain the emergence of conflicts of interest. Following this is the theory of nexus of contracts which introduces the coming together of two or more parties that execute a contract to achieve a certain objective. Since contracts cannot be fully and comprehensively written *ex ante*, "conflicts of interest" is likely to govern activities that lead to achieving pre-defined objectives. Agency theory introduces the principal-agent debate thus reiterating the problems of governance due to principal-agent conflicts. Berle and Means' firms that define managerial imperialism and the latest shareholder-stakeholder debate, further the theory of "conflicts of interest" to explain the emergence of corporate governance.

DISCUSSION QUESTIONS

1. "Separation of ownership and control is the root cause of all modern day governance problems". Explain.
2. "Conflicts of interest are primarily why we have governance issues". Do you agree?
3. "A firm is a nexus of contracts". Discuss.
4. What kinds of costs does the principal incur to align the interests of the agent with his own?
5. "Shareholders are also stakeholders of a corporation". Do you agree with this statement? If yes, explain the expectations a shareholder has from a corporation as against other stakeholders.

NOTES

1. See Berle, Adolf A. and Gardiner C. Means, (1932), *The Modern Corporation and Private Property*, New York, Macmillan Publishing Company for an interesting exposition.
2. Cochran, Philip L. and Steven I., Warwick, (1988), *Corporate Governance: A Review of Literature*, Financial Executives Research Foundation, New Jersey.
3. I refer to firms as Berle and Means firms, where there is a clear separation of ownership and control i.e., where the equity ownership is so widely diffused that no owner holds majority control of the firm and hence the firm is handed over to professional managers.
4. Studies by Eisenberg (1976), Demsetz (1983), Demsetz and Lehn (1985), Shleifer and Vishny (1986), Holderness and Sheehan (1988), Holderness, Kroszner and Sheehan (1999).
5. LaPorta, Rafael, Florencio Lopez-de Silanes and Andrei Shleifer, (1999), "Corporate Ownership Around the World", *The Journal of Finance*, Vol. LIV, No. 2, pp. 471–517.
6. "Incomplete contracts" implies that some actions would be taken and some rents would be paid ex-post. This leaves some space for re-contracting.
7. For a detailed analysis of incomplete contract theory, see Hart, O. and Moore, J., (1999), "Foundations of Incomplete Contracts", *Review of Economic Studies*, Vol. 66, No. 1, pp. 115–138.
8. For a pioneering work in the literature of agency theory refer to Ross, Stephen A., (1973) "The Economic Theory of Agency: The Principal's Problem", *American Economic Review*, Vol. 63, No. 2, pp. 134–139. However, the readers may please understand that not until the seminal article on agency theory by Jensen and Meckling in 1976 appeared was the agency theory able to establish itself as a contemporary theory to explain the nature of firms. The emphasis laid by Jensen and Meckling on agency costs in principal-agent transactions has come up as an alternative to explain the transaction costs proposed by the property-rights theorists.
9. A very serious paper that details how and in what ways agents can expropriate value from their principals has been authored by Turnbull, S., (2000), "Corporate Governance: Theories, Challenges and Paradigms", *Journal of Economic Literature*, Vol. 1, No. 1, pp. 11–43.
10. For a more precise understanding of the conditions that laid the foundations of managerial control in the United States, refer to an

interesting study, Mary, A. O'Sullivan, (2000), *Contests for Corporate Control: Corporate Governance and Economic Performance in the United States and Germany*, Oxford University Press: New York, pp. 70–145.

11. Prof. John Coffee Jr. argues on the contrary that during the nineteenth century when the largest business houses in the US and the UK converted into public–owned corporations, the laws in both the countries were not strong enough to protect minority shareholders. For a detailed explanation, refer to John C. Coffee Jr. (2000), "Convergence and its Critics: What Are The Preconditions to the Separation of Ownership and Control?" Working Paper No. 179. Columbia Law School, The Center for Law and Economic Studies, New York.
12. For a paper which delivers a political explanation to the rise of the Berle and Means firms in the United States and the weakness of the American social democracy, refer to Roe, J. Mark, (2000), "Political Foundations for Separating Ownership from Corporate Control", Working Paper No. 155, Columbia Law School, The Center for Law and Economic Studies, New York. In this paper, Roe argues, how if US had been more of a social democracy, later problems like incentive-alignments etc. would not have arisen.
13. In finance literature, such a problem is referred to as the 'free-rider problem.'
14. For an interesting study which quibbles with Roe's analysis of the role of political forces in the evolution of the Berle and Means firms, refer to Bainbridge M. Stephen, (1995), "The Politics of Corporate Governance: Roe's Strong Managers, Weak Owners", Research Papers No. 01–10, *Research Paper Series*, UCLA School of Law, Los Angeles.
15. In finance literature, shareholders are those who have direct pecuniary relationship with the corporation. They are part owners of the company. Their gains are measured in terms of the dividends or interest received by them. On the other hand, stakeholders are those who have either direct or indirect stakes in the corporation's business. Stakeholders can be as diverse as environment, society, consumers, suppliers, creditors, future generations etc.
16. For one of the most earliest works in understanding the role business has to play in society, refer to Howard R. Bowen, (1953), *Social Responsibilities of the Businessman*, Harper & Brothers: New York.
17. Residual risk here refers to the residual loss that the shareholder is likely to encounter in terms of reduction in his/her probable gains due to the agents' deviant behavior.

18. I refer to 'managerial myopia' in terms of the short-termist attitude of the managers, which, though it has major repercussions to the organizations at a later stage, is not taken into account while decision-making at contingent levels.
19. For more detailed discussion see Friedman, M., "The Social Responsibility of Business is to Increase Profits", in Beauchamp, L.T. and Bowie. E.N., (1997) edited *Ethical Theory and Business*, Prentice-Hall, New Jersey, pp. 56–61.
20. One of the most vocal proponents of stakeholder theory is Margaret Blair, an economist at the Brookings Institution. She argues that individuals invest in their own 'human capital' and this investment also leads to wealth generation. She contends that corporations must recognize the importance of human assets that are central to their success. For a clear understanding of her contention, refer to Blair, M., (1995), *Ownership and Control: Rethinking Corporate Governance for the Twenty-first Century*, Brookings Institution, Washington, DC.

Part II

Governance: Four Important Players

Chapter 3

Owners and Board

In the first section you have learnt what 'corporation' and 'governance' mean separately and then were introduced to the concept of corporate governance as well as the theories explaining the evolution of the current-day notion of corporate governance. While there are a variety of stakeholders in the governance process, we pick only four of them—owners, board, CEO and institutional investors, for the purpose of the book. In this chapter, owners and board are dealt with and Chapter 4 deals with CEOs and institutional investors.

OWNERS

Having understood the meaning of a corporation and its raison d'etre, it is time for us to understand the one who owns the corporation. There are varied views on who owns organizations. While shareholder theorists believe that owners are those who hold the shares of the corporation, stakeholder theorists argue that all constituents that hold a stake in the corporation for e.g., shareholders, society, future generations etc. can be termed as its owners.

Corporations do not exist in isolation. On a daily basis, they touch the lives of numerous stakeholders. While the shareholders reserve the right to maximize their gains, they cannot shrug off their social responsibility. Assume a situation where the owners of a corporation have built a road connecting two different parts of the town, on their property. What if they restrict the residents of the town from using that road? While they may be legally within their rights to regulate the movement on their roads, they have some responsibility towards nurturing a healthy society. Stakeholder theorists have thus advanced arguments that society, employees, future generations and other non-shareholder stakeholders can lay claim to the ownership of such corporations.

However, for the purpose of this book, we may reckon an owner as someone who has legal possession of some property. Ideally, such owners have the right to use their property the way they would want to and also regulate someone else's use of such property. This, in economic parlance, is called the right to exercise residual control over the property.

Finance literature defines owners as those investors who expect returns from their investments in lieu of the risk that they get exposed to by remaining invested in business. Ownership thus, in a way, refers to the cash flow right or the right to claim dividends.

Ownership of a firm also refers to the distribution of equity with regard to votes and capital. It identifies the equity owners and the controllers of the firm. In simpler terms, an owner is the possessor of some property (equity) and ownership is the assertion of the possession of that property.

It is common knowledge that promoters of firms are wealth-constrained. They cannot fund their businesses interminably. As a firm grows, the need for capital balloons up and promoters have very little choice other than to invite outside equity participation. Equity investors can come in various forms and sizes. The new owners define the character of the governance model the company should adopt. If too many investors including retail investors come on board, the company has diversified ownership, whereas if large investors join in with block holdings, the company will have concentrated ownership.

In either case, there are governance issues. These issues are explained in detail under Market-centric governance model and Relationship-oriented governance model in Chapter 5 with respect to diversified and concentrated ownership structures.

A listed corporation can have a wide range of owners, for e.g., promoter-owner, public or retail shareholders, employees and managers (through ESOPs), financial institutions, foreign shareholders, corporate bodies etc. Let us have a look at a typical shareholding pattern as filed by listed Indian companies in their annual reports (Table 3.1).

Table 3.1 *Typical Representation of Owners of a Corporation*

Indian Promoters	Individuals/Hindu Undivided Family; Central Government/State Government(s); Bodies Corporate; Financial Institutions/Banks
Foreign Promoters	Individuals (Non-Resident Individuals/Foreign Individuals); Bodies Corporate; Institutions
Public Shareholding: Institutions	Mutual Funds/Unit Trust of India; Financial Institutions/Banks; Central Government/State Governments(s); Venture Capital Funds; Insurance Companies; Foreign Institutional Investors; Foreign Venture Capital
Public Shareholding: Non-Institutions	Bodies Corporate; Individual shareholders holding nominal share capital up to Rs.1 lakh; Individual shareholders holding nominal share capital in excess of Rs. 1 lakh; Trusts; Non-Resident Individuals; Overseas Corporate Bodies
DRs	Shares held by custodians against which depository receipts have been issued

From the list above, owners can be regrouped broadly into five different categories: foreign investors, institutional investors, insiders, corporate bodies and public/retail shareholders. How each ownership group reacts to the corporation's business needs, throws light on the corporate governance practices followed by the corporation.

While not all shareholders listed in the table above would be running the business on a daily basis, the right to residual claims is reason enough for them to influence the management through their representatives elected to the board of directors. Of the shareholders listed above, the promoters run the day-to-day affairs of the business with help from professionals. How aligned such professionals are about the shareholders' interests is the premise on which the theories of corporate governance stand.

Ownership Structure

Jensen and Meckling have pared ownership structure into three identifiable variables. They assert that for any given firm, there are three different owner types: (i) inside equity (held by managers); (ii) outside equity (held by anyone outside of the firm); and (iii) debt (held by anyone outside of the firm).

Well-defined ownership structures define the boundaries of the firm as well as make it convenient for jurisprudence to make such issues as anti-trust, easy to comprehend and act on.

By ownership structure I mean the identity of the owners holding different ratios of the stock of the corporation. Through their holdings they draw proportionate amount of power to control the firm's activities. The governance of the enterprise largely depends on the authority exerted by the majority owners. Primarily, the control of the organization lies in the hands of the majority owner unless otherwise she dissociates from the residual control rights by separating ownership from control. In such cases, the party enjoying the residual control rights, controls the organization, and the other equity-owning parties either play an active role of monitoring or a passive role of dividend/return-expecting shareholders.

With the modern-day business becoming more and more complex in terms of capital needs, managing skills, employee behavior and the like, new types of equity owners have sprung from nowhere to assume control over organizations. Institutional investors like financial institutions, mutual funds, pension trusts, etc., for their own need to make profits, have started investing in other corporations. In a bid to own loyal employees, enterprises have begun doling out stock options to them. Managers have started holding companies through managerial equity.

Modern business is replete with diverse stockholding groups. As Thomsen and Pedersen in their paper "Industry and Ownership Structure", argue, these investors differ in terms of their wealth, risk aversion and the priority they attach to shareholder value relative to other goals.

Empirical studies have divided "ownership concentration" by characterizing firms as manager-controlled and owner-controlled. Firms are said to be owner-controlled where the owners own over twenty percent equity. Though many researchers differ over the percentage of equity held by owners to qualify for owner-controlled definition, a majority studies have qualified 'managerial control' as one when the ownership concentration is so low that the largest shareholder holds from four to five percent to as high as twenty percent.

Different researchers have divided ownership structures in different ways to accommodate their empirical findings. Some of them are listed below.

Pyramids: A very control-centric ownership structure, pyramids are usually adopted by big business groups with a holding company controlling multiple subsidiaries which, in turn, control their subsidiaries and so on. Such a complex ownership structure gives enough leeway to the families or promoters to retain control over the firms in the pyramid, despite their low stakeholding in any of the firms.

Cross Ownership: Very typical of Japanese corporations, cross ownership refers to the owning of shares of partner companies. Such partner companies could be anywhere on the spectrum from backward value chain to the forward value chain. For example, a company can have exposure to its suppliers' equity and also have investments in a financial institution which is funding it. Studies reveal that about 70% of the Japanese listed firms are characterized by cross corporate ownership. This results in a high degree of ownership concentration and control is interlocked to an extent that decision making largely follows a consensus-seeking approach.

In a cross-ownership scenario, information asymmetries wane away as equity holders have advanced inside knowledge of the management's decisions, future roadmaps and strategies. Important information is shared with the cross corporate owners through channels like interlocking directorates and network meetings.

Employee Ownership: Employees too can have ownership in firms they are working for. While privately they can buy company shares from the stock markets, officially, they can hold shares through Employee Stock Option Plans (ESOPs). However, ESOPs can be obtained only if the firms they are working for have ESOP plans in place. ESOPs work as an incentive mechanism to align the employee's interests to the larger interest of the company. Such alignment is construed to help the employees become goal-directed and perform better for their own good, thereby maximizing the company's good.

Large Blockholders: Large blockholders can come in many forms. Any stakeholding entity that holds a substantial chunk of a firm's equity can be termed as a large blockholder. Institutional investors, by virtue of their huge exposure to a firm's shares, are the most commonly known large blockholders.

Large blockholders play a very important role in shaping the direction of a firm's endeavors. They can contain the self-serving behavior of managers and play a proactive monitoring role. Unlike the small investors who vote with their feet, the large blockholders make good use of the "voice" or "exit" option to harness erring managers. In either case, the impact is huge. Firms where blockholders have voiced their dissent are rewarded negatively by the stock markets. Likewise, if the blockholders were to exit from the shareholding of the firm's equity, stock prices could take a huge beating since it is not easy to offload a substantial block of shares.

On the negative side, large blockholders can lower market liquidity thereby increasing the cost of capital. Managerial discretion can be seriously jeopardized with excessive monitoring, resulting in lower value extraction from business strategies.

Institutional Ownership: Pension funds, mutual funds, insurance companies and venture capital funds are typical institutional owners. They hold a substantial chunk of the ownership pie and in a way resemble the large blockholders. They do not engage in proxy fights nor do they elect members to the board of directors. However, their presence is usually construed to be a good indicator of the firm's health. Institutional owners punish errant firms by exercising the exit option thus negatively impacting share prices of the firm.

Retail Ownership: Individual shareholders are also known as retail shareholders. They are the weakest amongst the ownership constituents, as they wield very little influence on the business strategies of firms they have invested in. One usually does not find a representative of the retail investors on the boards of companies.

This ownership class is almost always deprived of information about the company's strategies. Their knowledge of and interest in remaining invested in firms is largely based on the news reports that are published in the yellow papers.

In a majority of the cases, individual investors adopt the "exit" option if they are not happy with the way their firms are operating. The "voice" option that is available to the large blockholders is not followed by the retail shareholders. The cost of voicing one's concern largely outweighs the benefits accrued off it.

Individual investors do not evince any interest in taking the deviant firms to task, as they feel that such an action by them could in a way lead other investors to freely ride on their efforts. This is known as the classic "free rider problem" in the finance literature.

Locus of Control

Studies done in the first few decades of the emergence of corporate governance literature were basically attempted at understanding whether separation of ownership and control really translated into weak or strong performance of the firm. The performance of the owners as against the managers was examined at length in many studies. While some researchers have clearly demarcated diversely held firms as manager-controlled, some have probed deeper to locate the locus of control—whether the firm is manager-controlled or owner-controlled. Corporate governance is primarily a function of the controllers of the firm. While there is a probability of the owners relinquishing control to the managers despite higher equity holdings, there is also a possibility that with lesser equity stakes the owners could still be controlling the corporations. Hence, the locus of control becomes central to understanding the way firms perform.

Manager-controlled Firms: This is a classic case of ownership dispersion. Shareholding is so diverse that no single ownership entity is in a position to take control of the firm. Research studies indicate that firms that are manager-controlled are usually the ones where ownership concentration is very minimal with the largest shareholder holding anywhere between four percent and twenty percent of the firm's equity. Managers end up controlling firms if ownership concentration does not reach a majority threshold.

Family-controlled Firms: Family-controlled firms are those that are managed and controlled by promoters and their families. In most cases, families hold a majority stake in the firm and individuals belonging to the families manage the firm. With their majority stake they are in a position to expropriate value from minority owners. A very simple yet powerful way of tunneling value is by rewarding themselves with high compensation. Since the control is with the family, agency costs are either non-existent or low.

Performance Arguments

Firm performance has often been measured against the backdrop of factors like ownership structure and locus of control. Popular literature lists seven arguments that explain the impact of ownership structure on the firm performance.[1] These arguments answer a lot of questions like: Why and to what extent do certain firms perform well? What kind of market conditions push managers to perform well? How, why, and to what extent does the locus of control help in a firm's performance? At what level of ownership do managers perform well?

Incentive Alignment Argument: Public corporations are defined by diverse stockholdership. Different types of stockholders entrust their hard-earned money to the care of managers. This may result in the manager expropriating value from the stockholders. Incentive alignment argument (also known as "convergence of interests" hypothesis) claims that corporate performance can be increased if the managers' interests are properly aligned with the interests of the shareholders. More equity ownership by the managers improves firm performance because of a better alignment of monetary incentives between the manager and other equity owners.

Takeover Premium Argument: Corporations that perform weakly become hot targets for takeovers. Takeover mechanism is an efficient instrument in the market for corporate control. Weakly performing companies command a low takeover premium which, in turn, affects the reputation of the managers or owners controlling them. Hence takeover premium argument proposes that more equity ownership by the manager/owner may increase corporate performance. With their higher stakes, they can repulse any hostile takeover bid from the market for corporate control and also compel the raiders in the market to pay higher takeover premiums.

Entrenchment Argument: Quite contrary to the above-mentioned arguments, entrenchment argument shows that high equity ownership by managers/owners might not always necessarily lead to an upward movement in the firm's performance. More equity ownership may decrease corporate performance due to two reasons. First, managers/owners may become complacent at high ownership levels in that they may not try to put in adequate efforts for the firm's growth. They may be so wealthy that they no longer intend to maximize profit. Second, with large ownership stakes, managers/owners may become so powerful that they may not need to consider other stakeholders' interests. They may instead expropriate shareholder value by pursuing their own desires like consuming extra perquisites, engaging in sweetheart deals, pursuing pet projects, trying to build empires and diversifying excessively.

Cost of Capital Argument: Liquid markets ensure lower interest rates thus bringing down the cost of the capital. A high amount of equity concentration with any kind of owner/stockholder implies that there is no market liquidity for the firm's holdings. Non-liquidity hampers diversification and other growth opportunities for the firm. This phenomenon leads to an increase in the cost of the capital thus decreasing corporate performance. Hence this argument proposes that high equity concentration by the owner/manager decreases corporate performance because it raises the firm's cost of capital.

Efficient Monitor Argument: As seen in the agency costs argument, managers try to expropriate shareholder value by creating information asymmetries. This increases the agency costs and hence brings down corporate performance. The manager/owner though derives personal benefits at the cost of other stockholders. Efficient monitor argument suggests that large owners or block owners because of their high stakes in the firm put in enough efforts to monitor and control the management thereby contributing to corporate performance.

Stulz's Integrated Theory: Stulz integrates the two models of takeover premium argument and entrenchment argument into a single theory. High equity ownership by the manager/owner may increase corporate performance. He presents a formal model that predicts a roof-shaped relation between managerial ownership and performance.

Morck et al's Combined Theory: Similar to the integrated theory of Stulz is Morck et al's combined theory in which they integrate the incentive alignment argument and the entrenchment argument into a single theory. Their findings suggest that at low levels of managerial ownership incentive alignment argument dominates entrenchment argument. As managerial holdings rise between zero percent and five percent, firm performance increases reinforcing incentive alignment hypothesis. However, further growth from that point to twenty-five percent ownership lowers the performance of the firm suggesting entrenchment. Again a rise of ownership above twenty-five percent level increases corporate performance though much more slowly.

In Conclusion

Whether ownership structure affects the firm performance is largely subject to where the locus of control is and to what degree the control is effective. While owners could own equity, they might not perform well if the locus of control is with the mangers or some extraneous party and similarly, they might not perform well if the degree of control wielded by them is lesser than any other stakeholder. The same argument applies to the other stakeholders too, in relation to their impact on firm performance.

BOARD OF DIRECTORS

Recall our discussion from the previous chapters that the source of today's corporate governance problems lies in the premise of separation of ownership and control. The professional managerial class has, by and large, taken control of corporations from the promoters, leading to the conflicts of interest theory. Managers may be self-serving and may take decisions that do not maximize shareholder wealth. To circumvent this problem, the shareholders appoint a board of directors that is primarily responsible to control the management's self serving behavior even while directing it to engage in shareholder wealth maximization activities.

In the words of Dehaene et al. "The board of directors is an important entity in a company, creating a link between shareholders and managers and therefore playing an important role in the governance of a firm."[2]

Boards are constituted of individuals who are elected by the shareholders for defined time periods. Usually companies elect directors on a rotating system so that at no given point in time is the entire board up for election. A fraction of the directors keep retiring every year and new members are either elected to the board or extension is given to the retiring directors. Board members can be removed from office either through a shareholder resolution or in some cases through a resolution by other members of the board.

The directors choose one of the members to officiate as the chairman/chairperson of the board. In smaller enterprises, the board of directors and the promoters are usually the same people and hence the board does not assume its true roles and responsibilities. However, in larger enterprises, there is division of power with the board assuming a supervisory role and leaving the company to be managed by professionals.

For their services, the directors are paid an annual salary in addition to the sitting fees for each meeting they attend. In some cases, the directors are also given stock options. While it is not a good idea for the directors to have any ownership in the company, as they too get entrenched like the management and end up taking myopic decisions, stock ownership is considered to be an incentive to contribute productively to the affairs of the company.

The board of directors is primarily responsible for protecting shareholder assets and ensuring that shareholders receive a decent return on their investments. It is the duty of the board to promote good governance practices like that of accountability and transparency. Enterprises that have boards actively promoting good governance not only attract value investors but also command a premium in the stock markets.

What a Director Should Not Do?

At a very broad level, a country's legal system defines the roles and responsibilities of the board of directors. However, companies can have a super-arching set of responsibilities in which the mandated legal responsibilities are subsumed. Directors are required to follow the mandated responsibilities with a high degree of prudence, loyalty and faith. It is important that directors do not engage in value-diminishing activities and not behave in ways that can be regressive for their firms.

Three examples of how the directors should or should not behave while discharging their duties are listed below.

Bias: Directors should not be biased while reviewing, evaluating or approving items brought to them for their verdict. They should not be burdened with pre-conceived notions which could have a negative bearing on direction setting.

Good Faith: They should exercise their powers in good faith. Directors should ensure utmost caution in not diverting the company's resources to their relatives and by not breaching their contracts. They should also be careful in not divulging confidential company information to competitors.

Avoid Serving Conflicting Interests: Directors should not engage in such activities or transact with such people or institutions where their interests conflict with the interest of the companies that they serve. In other words, they should not serve competing companies, nor should they in their private capacity compete with the company they are serving. They should always serve in the best interests of the company.

Types of Directors

Board composition plays a major role in defining the way a business is influenced and conducted. Boards are composed of different types of directors basically falling in the three major categories—executive, non-executive and independent.

Insiders: Promoters or their relatives and employees that have retired from the firm but have close ties with the promoters are considered as insiders.

Such directors are in a stronger position to create information asymmetries and expropriate minority shareholder wealth. Their dominance in the boards can be seen through higher use of accounting-based performance measures and minimal or low CEO influence.[3]

Executive Directors: Directors who are serving the company in a managerial capacity are called executive directors. They can also be termed as insiders. Technically, they are the most competent directors as they have inside knowledge of the complexities and the functioning of the company. However, this in itself can help them create information asymmetries and avoid scrutiny by the full board.

Affiliate Directors: These are directors that have some degree of business relationship with the company. They are not full-time employees of the company but share some business ties with it, be it in the form of providing consulting services to it or representing it legally or having invested in it.

Independent Directors: Independent directors are those that do not have a direct association with the company nor are they employees of the company. They are not former executives of the company nor are they on board to protect the interests of some third party. Such directors are believed to be advocating the shareholders' interest as they have no vested interest in the company. The assumption here is that independent directors are under no managerial obligation or pressure to cater to the CEO's whims and fancies. The depth of independent directors is measured by the exposure and experience that they have in their connection with other unrelated companies. Directors on the board of multiple 'unconnected/unrelated' companies across different industry verticals bring in more variety, diversity and rigor to the governance process. They also have the incentive to monitor management better than other directors, as they have their reputations to protect in the external "director labor" market.

Independent directors on the board bring in the needed expertise and objectivity that can, to a large extent, mitigate problems of managerial entrenchment and expropriation of shareholder wealth. They are also likely to detect financial frauds and plug them before they blow up into full-size scams.

Board Roles

There is a vast literature that identifies a variety of roles to be performed by the board of directors. From reviewing and approving organizational objectives to controlling the self-serving behavior of managers, from playing an oversight role to ensuring that stakeholder interests are not compromised, the board of directors engages in a variety of roles that help in improving the corporate governance of enterprises.

While there are many loose classifications of board roles, the most widely classified ones are that of (a) service role; (b) control role; and (c) strategic role.

Service Role: This classification follows the stewardship theory, and the board is considered a vehicle to enhance the image of the enterprise to the external world. The board of directors has to thus play a major role in working around improving the reputation of the enterprise they represent. They have to provide proper advice and counsel to the top management as and when required. It is also incumbent upon them to communicate with the company's stakeholders from time to time and brief them about the company's performance.

In its service role, the board has to co-opt services from its contacts for the benefit of the company it is serving. If the company needs funds and is unable to tap sources, the directors can help the company raise funds through their personal external influence. Likewise, whenever the company is in a sticky situation and the management is unable to handle it, the directors can provide their services by helping the company sail through the problem. As Mintzberg suggests, be it procuring crucial inputs like raw materials and external talent or raising funds when needed, the boards are obligated to provide first-rate services to the companies they are serving.[4]

Control Role: Markets judge the contribution of the boards based on the control they wield on self-serving managers. This role follows the tenet of agency theory, the common argument of which is that managers are agents of the principals and they can appropriate the wealth of the principals by creating information asymmetries. It is the responsibility of the boards to ensure that "conflicts in interest" is reigned in and the shareholders' interests are safeguarded.

It is the duty of the board to appoint a competent CEO and approve his/her compensation. The board must continuously monitor his/her performance and discipline him/her should there be any deviations. It is also responsible to fire or replace poorly performing CEOs. In practice, firing a CEO is a difficult task though. A study by Weisbach suggests that companies that have over 60% independent directors are more likely to fire non-performing CEOs as compared to other boards.

Sometimes, CEOs in a bid to maximize their authority, end up in mindless acquisition pursuits. The board must take an objective view of all the strategic decisions of the CEO and periodically review his/her performance.

In its control role, the board must succinctly review and challenge the CEO's assumptions and analysis. However, this does not mean that at every opportunity it should infringe upon the management's discretion.

Crucial managerial decisions should be scrutinized thoroughly and vetted by the BoD and wherever needed, rectify the business decisions. The board is not only responsible for reviewing and approving the enterprise's financial statements but is also responsible for evaluating and approving the percentage of dividends to be given to the shareholders.

Boards also have to establish audit, compensation and nomination committees. In some cases, boards establish an ethics committee in addition to the aforementioned committees.

Strategic Role: In its strategic role, the board plays the role of an elder statesman. It is the duty of the board of directors to guide the management in articulating the enterprise's vision and mission. It should be aware of the environmental factors and keep a keen watch on industry trends so as to make informed suggestions to the top management.

The board also assumes the responsibility of helping the management with resource allocation. Managers can be very myopic in decision making given their entrenchment in business. It is the board that brings in objectivity and infuses the external view thereby ensuring that resources are not allocated to non-productive or non-value adding projects.

While in its control role the board is responsible for course corrections, in its strategic role the board helps the management to develop, implement and monitor an enterprise's strategies. Acquisitions, mergers, demergers, share dilution—all such strategic moves have to be compulsorily vetted by the board of directors.

Board Attributes

Board attributes have a huge impact on an enterprise's corporate governance. Board attributes relate to the different elements that boards are made up of. Corporate governance research documents and classifies board attributes into four aspects: composition, characteristics, structure, and process.

Board Composition: What is the size of the board i.e., how many members are on the board of directors of a company? How many of them are independent directors and how many, executive directors? How many of them belong to the founding family? Which other companies are the directors affiliated to? How many foreign directors are on the board versus the local directors? Is there any minority representation on the board of directors? What is the qualification of each director? How many years of experience does each director have? Such questions, when answered, tell a lot about the character and strength of the board.

Board Characteristics: What is the collective experience of the directors? Do the directors have any vested interests? Do they own any shares in the company? How long have they been directors in the current enterprise? Do they have any directorial experience outside the current enterprise? What kind of functional expertise do they bring to finance, general management, operations, or sales? Such occupational expertise can have a significant influence on the board's ability to monitor management behavior.

Boards that are constituted of a majority of executive directors have the incentive not to reveal negative information to the shareholders, thereby preventing stakeholder intervention.

Board characteristics can be further broken down into board independence, board meetings and agenda, size and performance.

Board Independence: Is the CEO of the company also its chairman? Does the company encourage such duality? If not, then is the chairman related to the promoters? What is the percentage of independent directors on the board? Are the board subcommittees chaired by independent directors?

Board Meetings and Board Agenda: Board meetings are very beneficial to the shareholders, as the board members meet to discuss and oversee the performance of the management. But how many board meetings are enough for effective corporate governance? There is no perfect answer to this. Frequency of board meetings, many researchers believe, is largely dependent on the performance of the company. On an average, boards meet anywhere between six and eight times a year. Boards meet more frequently when the company performs poorly as against when it performs well. Thus board meetings are more reactive than proactive in nature.

The problem, though, is the directors often fail to do justice to their roles given the limited time that they have to discuss multiple items on the board agenda. The most common problem is that the CEO often sets the board agenda and is thus in a position to create information asymmetries. While the executive directors are in the thick of action and would easily comprehend the items on the agenda, the outside directors may not be in a position to take any meaningful decisions on important items as most of their time would be absorbed by routine tasks.

Board Size: The board size plays a very important role in the oversight function. While smaller boards are considered to be more effective in monitoring by containing process losses, bigger boards bring with them the necessary breadth and depth to monitor managerial performance effectively. In bigger boards, work can be distributed across a bigger number of reviewers thus making it easier for the full board to take crucial strategy decisions. However, bigger boards can become a liability given the level of coordination needed amongst the different directors while striving for a consensus on strategic issues. This can, in turn, help the CEO's dominance of the board.

Board Performance: Like the management, boards too need to perform. Boards are accountable to the shareholders and therefore it is incumbent upon them to partake in the management of the enterprise, albeit indirectly. Boards have to demonstrate their effectiveness in their stewardship function through oversight and control of management performance. Has the board's intervention helped in improving the profitability of the enterprise or has it helped it sustain the existing level of growth during turbulent times? How has the board been able to influence the social responsiveness of the enterprise? How is the company perceived by the customers and stakeholders—as ethical or unethical? Such perceptions have a direct bearing on the image the boards are cultivating. Has the board been effective in smoothly transitioning power to the new CEO who has replaced the outgoing CEO? How has it performed in terms of succession planning? In a nutshell, board performance is adjudged by the ability of the directors to perform their roles both as members of subcommittees and that of full boards, and also their efforts in achieving bringing about transparency in the company's performance by releasing timely and complete information to the shareholders.

Board Structure: Not to be confused with board composition, board structure relates to the way the board is organized. Does the board have a mix of director groups—independent, outside and executive? Are there any subcommittees for e.g., nomination committee, remuneration or compensation committee, and audit committee? If yes, are such committees chaired by non-executive or independent directors? In case such committees are chaired by executive directors, are there a majority of non-executive directors in the team? Is the board a single-tier board as followed by the market-based economies or is it a double-tiered one as followed by the relationship economies, for e.g., Germany? What role do the BoDs play in subsidiary companies and their boards? Is the CEO also the chairman of the company?

Board Processes: A board is as good as its processes. Processes are set for the board of directors to interact with each other at certain frequencies. How many times were board meetings conducted and whether directors attended such meetings? How effectively could the board of directors give broad directions to the management? Did the board follow a process to evaluate the management's performance? Is documentation of all board proceedings done appropriately? Do the directors arrive at a consensus while taking decisions? Does the board succeed in detecting the shortcomings in the CEO's strategies or does the CEO manage to hoodwink the board? Do the subcommittee members follow proper guidelines while auditing, screening and approving CEOs, approving relevant management items and while deciding on compensations? Questions like these throw sufficient light on how robust the board's processes are.

Board Committees

There are multiple types of subcommittees of the board. However, the most prominent ones—audit committee, compensation committee and nomination committee—are mandated by law.

Audit Committee: Audit committees are responsible for reviewing and checking the accuracy of the company's financial statements. It is the duty of the audit committee to select and recommend an external audit firm to the full board. While hiring the external auditor, care must be taken in ensuring that the audit firm or any of its members do not have any vested interests in the company and that they are independent of the senior management of the company. The committee has to liaise with the audit firm and periodically review the quality and stringency of internal accounting, audit procedures and financial statements. They should also ensure that not a single financial item is misrepresented in the annual reports or disclosure forms. It is their bounden duty to provide reliable and credible financial information to their shareholders.

Compensation Committee: Also known as the remuneration committee, it is the job of the compensation committee to set compensation norms for the entire company. Setting up base compensation, deciding on the CEO compensation, awarding stock options to employees, fixing incentive schemes and bonuses are all done by the compensation committee. Of late, the CEO compensation has become a major sore point with shareholders crying hoarse on the excessive remuneration being doled out to them by the compensation committees. How effective the committee is largely depends on the degree of independence they bring to the table. If the committee members are obligated to the CEO for their directorships, they are obviously bound to make benevolent decisions in favor of the CEO.

Nomination Committee: The nomination committee is primarily responsible for nominating new directors to the firm. The committee (i) identifies candidates qualified to serve as directors, and/or (ii) calls for nominations to the directorships that are open for the next elections and recommends to the full board to consider the nominees for appointment as directors. Such nominations are then put through an election process in the shareholders' annual general meeting. Only individuals who are approved by the shareholders during the annual meeting can become directors. However, it must be noted that in most cases, candidates for directorships are suggested by the CEO or the promoter and the nomination committees in reality lack the independence to follow the nomination of best practices.

In addition, the nomination committee is responsible for identifying, hiring, retaining, setting compensation levels and terminating search firms should such firms be employed by the firm to identify candidates for directorships. The committee is also responsible for conducting all necessary background checks of the potential candidates.

Board Evaluation

Board evaluation is an important function to assess how the boards have performed in their fiduciary responsibility. Board evaluations help the boards to identify the sources of failure and come out with plausible solutions to overcome them. Evaluations are to be done both for the full boards and the subcommittees. It is important that uncomfortable questions be asked by the board members of themselves before a crisis strikes the company.

Just like the management, the directors are also under pressure to perform. Bad reputation can dilute their equity in the external director-labor markets. Hence, it is desirable for them to be evaluated for their performance.

Objectives of Board Evaluation: Boards have to spell out clearly what they intend to achieve with their own evaluation. While the primary purpose of such evaluation would be to prove to the management and the shareholders their relevance and commitment to the organization, they should have a defined set of objectives that they intend to evaluate. Say, for example, questions like—is the board size justifying the governance needs of the organization? Are the subcommittees performing as per their mandate? How effective have the board members been in board meetings? Do the board members have the necessary skills and expertise to provide professional directorial services? Is the quality of board-management relationship strong enough to avoid confrontations on major strategy-related issues?

Targets for Evaluation: Once the objectives are defined, the board has to form a committee that would conduct the evaluation impartially. Targets for evaluation have to be identified based on the objectives of evaluation; say, for example, a particular member's contribution to the board has to be evaluated, or the effectiveness of the audit committee in evaluating financial statements has to be gauged. The evaluation committee members may also be targets of this evaluation.

There are innumerable benefits of board evaluation. For example, one can gain clarity on individual members' roles and responsibilities; the board as a whole can assume organizational leadership and provide better direction to the management; channels of communication open up between the board members and there is exchange of more meaningful information amongst them; and the board becomes more responsible, more accountable and more transparent in its conduct.[5]

SUMMARY

In this chapter, we looked at two of the four important stakeholders in the governance process—the owners and the board. While the owners fund the corporation and keep it afloat, the board plays a fiduciary role and also attempts at aligning the interests of the managers with that of the owners.

Empirical literature suggests that firm performance is largely dependent on one single factor—the locus of control. To decipher the degree to which owners impact the performance of the firm, it is important for one to understand with whom the "control" is vested with—the owner or the manager.

Boards play a major role in directing and shaping the governance practices of corporations. The subcommittees within the larger board indicate the seriousness with which boards approach the governance process. Only when boards actively participate in the broader level decision making and carry out their stewardship role in the right spirit, can corporations be properly governed.

DISCUSSION QUESTIONS

1. Who is an owner? List the different kinds of owners of a publicly listed corporation.
2. Define ownership and explain the different types of ownership structures.
3. What is meant by locus of control? Manager-controlled vs. Family-controlled firm. Which is better and why?
4. List the different types of directorships and explain them in detail.
5. Explain the different kinds of roles that a board plays.
6. Is it mandatory to have subcommittees of the board? If yes, what kinds of committees are common? Discuss.
7. "Chairman-CEO duality is a bane to good corporate governance". Discuss.

NOTES

1. Henrik Mathiesen has done extensive research in distilling the extant ownership-performance literature into these seven arguments. His website www.encycogov.com lists all these arguments in detail.
2. Dehaene A., De Vuyst V., and Ooghe Hubert, (2001), *Corporate Performance and Board Structure in Belgian Companies, Long Range Planning*, Vol. 34, Issue 3, pp. 383–98.
3. Bousmosieh, A.S. and Reeb, D. M., (2009), "Inside Directors, Managerial Competition and the Asymmetric Information Problem", Working Paper Series. Available on http://papers.ssrn.com/sol3/papers.cfm?abstract_id=674082
4. Mintzberg, H., (1983), *Power In and Around Organizations,* Prentice-Hall.
5. Mishra, R.K. and Navin B., (2000), Corporate Governance and Public Enterprise Boards, Productivity, Vol. 40, No. 4, January–March, pp. 544–49.

Chapter 4

Chief Executive Officer and Institutional Investors

We have over the previous chapters discussed the notion of separation of ownership and control, time and again. You may also recall the discussion we had on managerial expropriation of shareholder wealth, information asymmetries, conflicts of interest and agency costs. The first part of this chapter is an extension of these ideas within the context of the role of management (or more precisely, the Chief Executive Officer) in the firm's governance process. The second part of the chapter discusses a very important player in the governance process—institutional investor. Of late, institutional investors are playing a major role in influencing the corporate governance practices of corporations. We discuss the kinds of institutional investors, their key characteristics and the role that they play in the governance process, in this chapter.

CHIEF EXECUTIVE OFFICER

For about a century now, we have been observing the rapid pace with which corporations are growing. As has been discussed in the previous chapters, need for more and more capital is concomitant with such growth and hence stocks in companies have come to be shared by a wide range and type of shareholders. Managers are predominantly in control of such widely-dispersed corporations.

It is common knowledge that management by virtue of being on hand, possesses more business information than the owners of the corporations. This helps them create information asymmetries which they may use to the detriment of the well being of the corporations they run.

Management's interests might not be in conjunction with the interests of the promoters or the shareholders. This conflict of interest could lead to some unpleasant situations in the general commandeering of the corporations. Also, smart managers find out ways to tunnel pecuniary benefits to themselves through excessive compensations and attractive retirals. The role of the management therefore is important not only because it is primarily responsible for the performance of the corporations it runs they but also because of its power to create and/or enjoy residual value.

Managerial behavior has been debated to a great extent even outside of the agency theory arguments. Refer to our discussion in Chapter 3 under Agency Theory to understand interest-alignment arguments. An interest-alignment incentive is just a positive reinforcement for better managerial behavior. Other than this, there are other constraints that keep a check on managerial behavior. For example, product market competition, takeover threats, existence of markets for managerial labor and non-availability of debts. Such constraints govern managerial behavior to a large extent.

Role of CEO

The chief executive officer is the most important figure in a company's strategic management process. The CEO heads the senior management in the day-to-day operational management of the company and is responsible for spelling out the organization's vision, mission and goals. He/she develops organizational strategies in such a way that organizational objectives are met and is also responsible for performing managerial functions like planning, organizing, controlling and leading. In a way this means that the CEO should be competent to not only analyze the external environment but also have the skills to make strategic choices at appropriate times.

The CEO has to handle and manage the demands and aspirations of a multitude of stakeholders such as suppliers, customers, employees, society, shareholders and boards. A good CEO has the right combination of conceptual, technical and human skills.

Some important roles are detailed below.

As a Leader: CEOs are first amongst equals and are leaders of leaders. In their leadership role, CEOs set a clear direction for their team and set the bottom line for executing, implementing and making things happen. CEOs also play the role of the chief motivator of the company and equip their team with the courage and talent to ward off any crisis that the company faces or is likely to face.

As leaders, CEOs have to possess a good mixture of the conceptual, technical and human skills. Effective leaders are those who have a strong followership not because of their position but because of their leading skills. Leaders who demonstrate their leadership skills by walking the talk earn a lot of respect from their team members.

In their leadership role, CEOs have to foster a culture of compliance and ensure that the individuals in the company are aligned with its mission, vision, values and objectives. Also they have to identify and promote talent and ensure that their successors as well as successors for their team members are identified and their careers appropriately planned. A good CEO will earnestly try to implement succession plan and groom leaders for the future.

As a Change Agent: The only thing that is constant in today's business is change. Change can be at many levels—organizational, unit or individual level. CEOs should be amongst the first employees to accept and embrace change. Further they have to act like change agents in implementing the change management process. Amongst the most difficult tasks, the real challenge lies in getting everyone in the organization to accept the change and strive towards achieving organizational objectives. A good CEO understands that change management is fraught with frustrations as there is usually a strong resistance to any kind of change. Good change agents do not drive the change in a top-down fashion but go about the change management process in a very systematic and well-defined manner. They ensure that "change" is communicated appropriately and timely to the stakeholders that are likely to be affected by the change and then implement the change in a way that would lead to lesser friction and greater organizational value.

As a Decision Maker, Monitor and Reviewer: Decision making is the biggest of all the CEO responsibilities. As decision makers, CEOs are supposed to take organizational decisions that can be implemented by their team. Also, they are the final approvers of all decisions made by the team members. The decision making role of the CEO entails that he/she formulate policies and present the same to the board for its consideration and approval.

Amongst other important responsibilities, CEOs have to constantly monitor the performance of the organization. They have to be on top of all the happenings and ensure that the leaders in their organization do not deviate from plans. Good CEOs keep an eye on the MIS of the company and ensure that they chair periodic operations and strategy meetings. For e.g., they can schedule a monthly operations meeting to monitor the operational performance of their reportees or a quarterly strategic meeting to check whether the goals set out for the quarter were met and what course of action should be taken in the subsequent quarter. The monitoring and reviewing responsibility of the CEO means that they have to be on their toes all the while and cannot have any respite as long as they are heading the organization.

As a Communicator: It is the bounden duty of the CEOs to ensure that communication flows within the organization are robust and working. Also, as leaders of the organization, they have to ensure that policy changes or any organizational level communication meant for the consumption of the larger employee groups percolate down and not get mired in excessive bureaucracy. A CEO's communication skills can be a great asset during the change management process. CEOs have to make a good story of the transformation process and communicate the same to the employees very effectively.

Apart from the employees, the CEOs interact with multiple stakeholders on a daily basis, be they board members, government, suppliers, banks, or investors. They should be extremely effective in communicating with each stakeholder in a business language that the stakeholder feels comfortable in. Also, they should provide timely, accurate and relevant information to each stakeholder as and when necessary.

As a company spokesperson, the CEO meets up with the media or engages in PR activities, whenever necessary. The CEO should be well equipped to communicate with external stakeholders without creating any controversies.

As a Resource Allocator: Resources are always in short supply in organizations and hence CEOs need to plan their work with resource constraints in mind. Resources can come in various forms—time, funds, space and key inputs amongst others. CEOs play the role of resource allocators in that they decide which projects or initiatives should the funds be committed to and in what proportions, which leaders from the senior management should be put on which projects and for what duration, what amount of their time should be allocated for which projects and for which discussions and also for which individuals.

As a Catalyst: In the multiple roles that CEOs play, they cannot shy away from their functional responsibilities. As executive leaders they have to share their knowledge with and make their services available to a variety of functions, be it human resource management, financial management, manufacturing, marketing or facilities.

CEOs have to play the role of catalysts in overseeing and approving the design of the products/services the company offers; ensure the product/service is appropriately marketed; contribute to enhancing the brand image of the company through their PR and organizational skills; encourage the HR leaders to adopt the best personnel policies to encourage cooperation and collaboration; take active interest in attracting, retaining and developing the right talent; create a work environment that is conducive to personal and professional growth of employees; oversee the budgeting process, and plan and recommend capital expenditures to the board; and ensure that financial reports comply to the statutory requirements.

CEO Duality

We have learnt from the previous chapter that the board of directors is led by the chairman. In most corporations, the chief executive officer also performs the role of the chairman of the board of directors thus leading to a duality in functions. Proponents of good corporate governance oppose this duality and seek for separation in these roles. They argue that such a duality would obviously lead to conflicts of interest thereby shaking the very foundation of corporate governance. By functioning as the chairman of the board of directors, the CEO can be in a position to decide on the quality and quantity of time needed for discussions on certain items. This may lead to creation of information asymmetries thereby hitting at the roots of good governance practices.

However, some researchers opine that duality can help organizations grow faster and better. An external chairman of the board of directors could scuttle the CEO's growth plans and could apply brakes where not necessary. Also, managerial initiative that is the prerogative of the CEO could be disturbed by the chairman's excessive interference in the name of strategic direction. Companies that do not have CEOs officiating as chairmen, can tend to become too conservative in their outlook and might not take enough risks thereby losing opportunities that the markets may offer.

CEO Compensation and Performance

Over the past two decades, executive compensation has skyrocketed to unprecedented proportions and is still rising. The compensation/remuneration committees of corporate boards are responsible for setting executive pay and it has often been seen that the CEOs' pay is very lucratively structured, and justification for such excessive payments are made by references to the market standards. There is a plethora of literature around the theme of CEO compensation and both academics and markets are now deploring the skyrocketing packages.

What is an appropriate compensation for the CEO? At what compensation levels are they motivated enough to deliver their best to the organization? Does CEO's compensation and firm performance have any relation at all? What if the compensation falls short of his/her expectations? Will he/she expropriate shareholder wealth? At what level of compensation can conflicts of interest be avoided and "convergence of interests" be promoted? There are no concrete answers to such questions. Firm performance is a function of multiple factors, CEO behavior being one amongst them. How far CEO compensation helps in "convergence of interests" thereby leading to a better firm performance is still a major point of discussion.

There are multiple viewpoints on the subject of CEO compensation with some maintaining that managerial shareholding helps in aligning the interests of the manager with that of the shareholders. Equity ownership pushes the managers to perform better for their own sake. Some authors however provide empirical evidence of no established relationship between managerial shareholdings and firm performance.

But Morck et al. in their empirical paper titled "Management Ownership and Market Valuation: An Empirical Study", suggest that an inverted U-shaped relationship exists between managerial shareholdings and firm performance. Firm performance drastically improves with managerial shareholdings, but after a certain threshold level, CEO's get entrenched and hence performance dips.

CEO compensations are not worked out in isolation. The board of directors is responsible for structuring the compensation package of the CEO. Critics of CEO compensation practices argue that the board of directors either turn a blind eye to the CEO's package, or play into the hands of the CEO who has the power to influence the board, or structure a package that fails in maximizing shareholder value. Also, in most cases, outside directors are usually hired and fired by the CEO and hence they refrain from antagonizing the CEO, even if CEOs were to structure their compensation packages as per their fancies.

Succession Planning

After the current CEO quits, who will replace him/her? Has the current CEO identified his/her right replacement? Has he/she groomed the new leader? Or will the new CEO be hired from outside the organization? Succession planning deals with such questions.

It is very important that organizations create backups of leadership candidates to mitigate issues related to leadership crisis. Senior leaders should take it upon themselves to periodically review their next level of leaders and identify their potential. Such identified candidates can be exposed to the work done by the seniors so as to ensure that they become able backups just in case there is a leadership void. Usually, it is observed that most companies do not take succession planning seriously which is why outsiders are scouted for as replacements to the outgoing leaders. Grooming internal leaders can be of great help in that it provides for a ready replacement market for managerial labor and the costs of external replacement for e.g., searching, hiring and acclimatizing costs, can be done away with.

In most cases, top management appointees are usually firm insiders and have a good understanding of the business of the firm and the industry. Dalton and Kesner in an interesting paper on organizational performance, suggest that external candidates are not hired unless they are presumed to be capable of bringing in exponential improvements in the functioning of the enterprise. Else, such hiring does not justify the costs involved in appointing outsiders. Also, if an outsider is selected for the CEO's position, stock markets tend to be circumspect and surmise that the firm is facing some serious problems.

The main objective of succession planning is to ensure that no right candidate is denied of his/her rightful place at an opportune time.

Managerial Myopia

A widely popular term in the governance literature "managerial myopia" reflects on the behavioral aspect of managerial decision making. CEOs are wary of the existence of a large market for managerial labor and hence most decisions they take are linked to the fear of being displaced. While governance philosophy suggests that CEOs take a long-term view of the corporations they are leading and take only such decisions that would maximize stakeholder value in the long run, market-driven fear coerces the CEOs to make short-term decisions that would stand to benefit them personally and considerably improve their equity in the managerial labor market.

Managerial myopia, therefore, refers to the manager's short-sightedness in taking decisions. Such myopic behavior can lead to inefficient investments that may hoodwink the stock markets and improve the corporation's short-run share price at the cost of long-term profits. The CEO can be very discreet in letting out information, and since he/she has the capability to create information asymmetries, he/she is well placed to play around with such information to the detriment of the corporation in the long run.

A myopic CEO would refrain from sharing any bad news with the stock markets. Instead he/she would distract the markets' attention by investing in projects that promise high ex-ante profits. Likewise he/she would resort to subterfuge by generating positive buzz around some project while taking a short-term decision on another project.

Stock markets are to blame for such myopic behavior. CEOs are forced to produce positive results quarter after quarter. Hence, CEOs are excessively focused on meeting their quarterly guidance rather than attempting any large-scale transformations. In a bid to appease the stock markets, CEOs engage in short-termist behavior thereby stealing the corporations of their long-term benefits. Another important factor for such myopic behavior could be the fact that the CEO's career is linked to the quarterly results. Negative results in a quarter can mean that the CEO is inefficient. To disprove this inefficiency theory, CEOs engage in activities that are beneficial to their careers but are detrimental to the long-term health of the corporations they lead.

INSTITUTIONAL INVESTORS

Corporate scandals across economies, particularly that follow the Anglo-Saxon model of governance, have received a great deal of attention in recent times. More and more shareholders are bearing the brunt of inefficient management of companies. Shareholder value is getting eroded like never before. *Why*? Recall our discussion on Berle and Means hypothesis in the earlier chapters. As organizations are growing in size, their reliance on shareholders for their funding needs is increasing. Markets are getting increasingly stormed by retail shareholders. But do the retail shareholders with their small shareholding have the motivation, incentive or power to play an active role in monitoring managerial performance? *No.* The agency cost of monitoring managerial behavior is way too high for a small shareholder. Also, there is always the possibility of free riders making the most of an individual shareholder's efforts. So where do the households interested in maximizing their savings go to?

In the last decade and a half, 'institutionalization of savings' has emerged as one of the biggest developments of the financial markets. Household savings which were otherwise individually invested into the stock markets is now being channelized through institutional investors. The growth of mutual funds and insurance companies in emerging economies like India and the unprecedented growth of pension funds in the Anglo-Saxon economies have reaffirmed the important role that institutional investors are playing in the financial markets. As an OECD report suggests "Institutional investors exercise a dominant influence on developments in primary and secondary securities markets, in the money market and in the foreign exchange market. They dominate a substantial part of securities trading in both cash and derivative markets. They also influence the development of fund management and risk management securities."[1]

Who Are Institutional Investors?

There are various definitions of institutional investors but the common thread underlying all the definitions is the fact that there are multiple individual investors who prefer holding stock through a professional investment organization with the understanding that such an entity has expert knowledge in the way funds operate and that it works towards maximizing the gains of the individual investors.

Some authors have defined institutional investors as:

Organizations which raise funds from individuals and corporation and invest, as principle in the stock markets, using professional management and operating within the constraints provided by their own articles and trust deeds and tax and legal considerations.

Briston and Dobbins

Institutional owners are radically different shareholders from the dedicated individual investor.

Hugh Sherman and C. Rajeshwara Rao

Davis E Philip and Benn Steill in their book *Institutional Investors,* have defined institutional investors as "specialized financial institutions which manage savings collectively on behalf of small investors, towards a specific objective in terms of acceptable risk return maximization and maturity of claims."[2]

The term "institutional investor" is defined as a company with multiple owners, that is interested primarily in portfolio investments, and which derives revenue from dividend income and/or realized capital gains from asset sales.

Boyan Belev

Categories of Institutional Investors

Pressure Sensitive: Such investors typically go along with management decisions since they are likely to have potential or current business relations with the company they have invested in. They try to avoid jeopardizing their relationship with the company by voting against management decisions. Banks and insurance companies can be categorized as pressure sensitive institutional investors, especially because of their ongoing relationship with the firms they have invested in.

Pressure Insensitive: Pressure insensitive institutional investors do not have any relationship with the companies they have investments in. They prefer voting against management decisions and exercise their monitoring role to the hilt. Pension funds are typical examples of pressure insensitive institutional investors. They invest in firms with a certain philosophy and are far more concerned about the value that they can provide to their stakeholders than be entrenched in any relationship with the firm.

Types of Institutional Investors

There are a variety of financial intermediaries who qualify as institutional investors. Though they go by different names like pension funds, portfolio investors, mutual funds and so on, they are basically asset management companies that act as small investors' fund and risk aggregators.

Pension Funds: Pension funds have in the past decade and a half emerged as the new financial intermediaries. In many countries, they operate as the largest institutional investors given the large amount of funds they are capable of investing in the stock markets.

Davis has defined pension funds as "forms of institutional investor, which collect, pool and invest funds contributed by sponsors and beneficiaries to provide for the future pension entitlements ofbeneficiaries."[3]

Pension funds relate to a financial vehicle established by the employer where both the employee and the employer park their retirement contributions to help employees draw a pension post retirement. In India, pension funds do not access capital markets for fear that investments, if lost in the stock markets, could jeopardize families of the retirees.

Portfolio Investors: Portfolio investors are those that hold securities or other financial assets of foreign companies or foreign governments, or acquire assets in foreign countries without actively engaging in either the management or the oversight role. They can be classified as passive investors.

Mutual Funds: Mutual funds are, as the name suggests, funds pooled and raised mutually by a wide group of people for the purpose of investing in financial market instruments, be they corporate bonds, stocks, or any other type of securities or even public bonds issued by the State or Central governments. Such funds are professionally managed by asset management companies known as mutual funds.

Funds are raised by mutual fund companies by floating New Fund Offers, popularly known as NFOs post their examination of lucrative investment opportunities. Investors who believe in the investment opportunities identified by the mutual funds buy such NFOs and trust their funds to these professional fund managers.

Insurance Companies: Insurance companies are financial intermediaries that finance contingent losses of individuals by transferring the risk of such losses to a larger number of people. Insurance companies act as risk poolers by collecting premiums from different individuals and reimbursing those that have incurred losses.

Hedge Funds: Hedge funds are private investment funds that collect funds from high net worth individuals or high value investors and invest a part or all of their assets in publicly traded securities and attempt at minimizing the investors' market exposure through different types of hedging vehicles. The purpose of the hedge funds is to deliver maximum returns to the investors by investing in a diverse portfolio that has less risk and throws up stable returns. Hedge funds are basically instruments that offset other market risks by taking pre-decided positions with regards to risk exposure.

Other types of institutional investors are endowment funds, asset management companies, investment trusts, unit trusts.

Key Features of Institutional Investors

Despite the varying focus that different institutional investors have as far as their investment philosophy is concerned, there is a common thread to the larger set. From pooling risks to lowering monitoring costs, all types of institutional investors are characterized by the same set of features.

Risk Pooling: Small investors do not have the wherewithal or the incentive to monitor firm behavior in order to maximize their returns. Institutional investors provide a platform to pool the risks of such small investors thus providing a better trade-off of risk and return for their holdings. Since institutional investors are specialized investors, they are in a far better position to circumvent risk as against any individual investor.

Vehicles for Long-Term Savings: Individual investors looking for alternative avenues for saving their hard-earned money may entrust their monies to the institutional investors. Of late, institutional investors with their stable and higher rate of returns have emerged as the most preferred vehicles for long-term savings. While savings stagnate in banks and attract lower rates of interest, savings with the institutional investors are likely to throw up returns in line with the market movements. Market-aligned returns, though a bit risky, usually offer a better return on investments provided the individual investors takes a long-term view of such investments.

Ability to Process Information: Institutional investors have expert fund managers on their rolls. The fund managers have the needed expertise to comprehensively absorb and process information on firm performance and trends. They are, therefore, in a better situation to exercise "voice" or "exit" option as compared to the individual investor.

Liquidity Oriented: Institutional investors prefer liquidity to control. This is in concomitance with their business model where they have to take fiduciary care of their shareholders' and clients' interests. It is very important that institutional investors follow the cannon of liquidity as, unlike banks which are privy to private information, they have to rely on public information to take any crucial decisions. Such orientation is beneficial for the individual investors as they are assured of their investments being safe even in cases where they fail to generate decent returns.

Focus on diversification: Since institutional investors are custodians of small investors, their primary focus is on generating maximum return with the minimum risk possible. They do not trust all their funds to one industry sector or a single firm. Instead they adopt a diversified investment strategy that includes investing, following a risk-reward assessment of industry sectors and individual firms. Their diversification strategy could include investing in international capital markets too. Such kind of investment management is known as portfolio management in finance parlance.

Lower Costs: Due to their economies of scale, institutional investors are in a position to lower monitoring and transaction costs. Small shareholders thus stand to benefit from lower monitoring overheads as well as lesser advisory fee.

Role of Institutional Investors

Institutional investors have the power and influence to make or break a company. Unlike the small shareholder who has no or marginal incentive in monitoring the company's performance, institutional investors by virtue of their large shareholding can act as effective monitors of managerial performance. They very often exercise the "voice" or "exit" option available to them. They make themselves heard through their active participation in monitoring and directing management. In cases where they fail to constrain managerial excesses, they let their dissent known by voting through their feet, meaning, offloading their holdings in the stock market. Heavy institutional selling can send wrong signals in the marketplace with other investors too selling their stock, thereby further depressing share prices. Their philosophy of placing premium on fundamentals helps in efficient pricing of stocks.

Institutional investors, as agents of small shareholders, have the motivation to partake in the voting process and hence exercise a considerable influence on managerial decision making. However, some researchers argue that the institutional investors do not have the expertise to evaluate management decisions. Also, they may in some cases downplay the interests of their minority shareholders. Some others have suggested that institutional investors cannot afford to play an active role in the governance of corporations, as they face conflicts of interest that hold them from long-term representation on corporate boards. It is difficult for institutional investors to remain invested in corporations and play a "voice" role at the cost of investment liquidity.

The canon of loyalty dictates that the institutional investors take voting decisions in the best economic interests of the shareholders they represent. Small shareholders cannot vote since institutional investors act as intermediaries. Hence it is the duty of the institutional investors to vote against all value decreasing proposals.

Different institutional investors have different levels of focus. While some have short-term interest in the companies that they are invested in, some take long-term positions. Some institutional investors like pension funds, for e.g., CALPERS are very sensitive and hence adopt a very cautious approach in their relationship with the invested company. Institutional investors follow an investment philosophy that is guided by multiple parameters, i.e., the nature of the fund, the liabilities of the fund, regulatory and tax regimes such funds operate in, their asset dimensions or kinds of products—fixed income or equity income, international equity or domestic equity, etc.

Institutional investors invest in companies following a stringent selection screening. Also, they follow a more serious intervention strategy when firms they are invested in do not perform as per their standards. In the Anglo-Saxon economies, institutional investors have emerged as barometers of share price trends. They are playing a crucial role in effecting positive changes in corporate governance.

In their stature, institutional investors have overtaken banks in many ways. Unlike banks that engage in debt financing, institutional investors participate in equity financing and exercise their right to associate or dissociate with the company as per market circumstances. Also, their presence lends to regulating managerial expropriation of shareholder wealth.

Good institutional investors thus help in (i) reducing information asymmetries thereby controlling agency costs, (ii) increasing liquidity thereby enabling firms to dilute their equity for emergency funding, and (iii) introducing and improving best governance practices by playing an effective monitoring role.

Institutional Investors Should Be Proactive

Regulated banks are no more attractive destinations for individual savings. Today such savings have moved to the more lucrative institutional investment companies. Institutionalization of savings is by far the biggest paradigm shift in the world of firm financing. This has brought in a sea change in the way capital markets across the world function.

Countries are bracing up with new regulations to contain any inequities that are likely to be generated by the spawning of institutional investors. Since institutional investors are agents of the small shareholders, adequate care must be taken to regulate their investment behavior. The primary reason they are in the retail fund management business is due to the individual shareholder's inability to monitor firm performance and the fear of expropriation of their wealth. Institutional investors to a large extent stand fiduciary guarantee to erosion of shareholder wealth and hence it is incumbent upon them not to engage in any adverse selection of stocks or make any imprudent asset allocation decisions.

It is important that institutional investors make appropriate disclosures to their clients at all times. Such disclosures should relate to the companies that the institutional investor has invested in, the quality of assets, the quantum and nature of risks involved, the spread of such risks, and contractual obligations if any.

SUMMARY

In this chapter we have understood the role played by the chief executive officer and the institutional investors in the governance process.

CEO-chairman duality has serious shortcomings and any organization that swears by practicing good corporate governance should avoid such duality like a plague. And, while it is important that the CEO be constantly monitored for his/her value appropriation decisions, one should not forget that excessive interference or monitoring can stifle his/her managerial initiative that might coerce him/her to take myopic decisions. We are aware that managerial myopia has multiple shortcomings and can be detrimental to the organization in the long run.

Institutional investors are the face of the plethora of retail investors willing to partake the risk and wealth generated by modern-day corporations. They play a very important role in the governance process by voicing their dissent against managerial excesses. Of late, organizations are taking them seriously due to their ability to influence capital markets. They have emerged as indicators of organizational health, so much so, that their exit from an organization is construed as a signal of an impending bad performance by that organization.

DISCUSSION QUESTIONS

1. What role does a CEO play? Explain in detail.
2. Is CEO compensation related with performance? Explain.
3. What is managerial myopia? Cite some real world examples to substantiate your understanding.

4. Who are institutional investors? Pressure sensitive versus pressure insensitive institutional investors – which you think are better. Explain.
5. Discuss the different kinds of institutional investors.
6. "Institutional investment is better than retail investment". Do you agree? Explain.

NOTES

1. OECD (2003), Institutional Investors—Statistical Yearbook, 1992–2001. Available at http://www.oecd.org/document/23/0,3343,en_2649_34247_25495063_1_1_1_1,00.html
2. Davis E Philip and Benn Steill, (2001) *Institutional Investors*, The MIT Press, Cambridge, MA.
3. Davis E Philip (1995), *Pension Funds, Retirement-Income Security and Capital Markets: An International Perspective,* Oxford University Press.

Part III

Corporate Governance: Four Models

Chapter 5

Market-oriented and Relationship-based Models

While corporate governance has come to be synonymous with the widely held firms following Berle and Means' observations, literature documents the existence of three other governance models. Not all corporations are widely held. Shareholding in some is so intertwined that there is no scope for diverse shareholding. The type of governance model that corporations adopt is largely dependent on the country and economy they are operating in. A US- or a UK-based firm is expected to be diversely held. However, a Japanese firm is likely to be structured in the form of a *keiretsu*. In countries that are transitioning from State control to private control, shareholding may not be in the lines of either the United States or Japan. Likewise, corporations in emerging economies are in a constant state of flux as far as shareholding is concerned.

This chapter deals with two most widely established models of corporate governance—the market-oriented (Anglo-Saxonic) model and relationship-based (Germano-Nippon) model. Chapter 6 will take you through the other extant models of governance. Make a note of the economies such models operate in. You will realize that a country's economic fabric has a large bearing on the type of governance adopted by corporations within that country.

MARKET-ORIENTED GOVERNANCE MODEL

Market-centric economies are largely characterized by a diffusion of equity ownership across a cross-section of shareholders. Due to reasonably good investor protection, capital markets are strong and liquid. Shareholders, therefore, diversify their portfolio holdings over a wide range of corporations. Thus none of the shareholders are in a position to control the corporation through their ownership stake. Hence, professional managers are hired to run the corporations on behalf of the scattered shareholders. The primary benefit of such a model is the easy agglomeration of capital and the wider spread of shareholder risk.

This model of corporate governance is beset with myriad problems yet is considered successful by many. Scandals in world-class companies like Enron, Tyco International, Adelphia, Worldcom, ImClone, Grubman/Citigroup and GE have exposed the futility of such a model. While, on the one hand, the model is characterized by the existence of a strong market for corporate control and ready managerial labor, on the other hand, insider trading and excessive executive compensation seem to be regular features.

Governance problems arise when the managerial class create information asymmetries and expropriate shareholder value. Since ordinary shareholders are distanced from management because of their fractionated ownership, the managerial class that directly oversees day-to-day operations of the firms is in a position to create information asymmetries. All information that would benefit them personally would be guarded secretly and all such information that is of no material benefit to them may be relayed to the shareholders and other external parties. Hence, to align the interests of the managers with those of the shareholders, agency costs have to be incurred. Refer to the explanation under Agency Theory in Chapter 2 to understand the constituents of agency costs.

In a bid to maximize their personal benefits, managers adopt a short-term approach. Managerial myopia is largely a function of active capital markets. Capital markets reward those who perform well in the short term and managers are not oblivious to the fact that trading off long-term sustained growth for short-term instant returns would reap them rich dividends. Hence all their actions are directed towards maximizing short-term profits. This leads them to take decisions that deplete shareholder value.

Managers try to increase the size of the firm through acquisitions and mergers so as to artificially improve profits and hence improve their compensation packages. The distance created by the separation of ownership and control in the market-oriented firms enables managers to pursue their own goals of non-value maximizing activities. Bad acquisitions that could be an onus on the corporation at a later date might be made now because the benefits to be accrued from such acquisitions may seem lucrative. Managerial hubris attached with the power gained through managing huge empires, spells doom to the shareholder value.

Another governance problem arises when independent directors are nominated by the Chief Executive Officer of the corporation. Independent directors thus nominated remain loyal to the CEO and the corporation is run as per his/her whims and fancies. The board of directors which is elected by the shareholders to oversee the working of the executive, remains a mute spectator to the executives' decisions out of sheer loyalty to the CEO. This misalignment of the interests of the board of directors as well as the managerial class with the shareholders' interests creates corporate governance problems.

Regulatory bodies like the Securities and Exchange Commission (US) and Securities and Exchange Board of India (India) and other such country-specific regulators have tried to mitigate such problems through their punishment provisions. However, the effectiveness of such provisions is questioned, given the fact that the most reputed corporations are expropriating shareholder value right under the nose of these regulators.

Markets, however, have devised their own tools and techniques to alleviate corporate governance problems. The existence of the market for corporate control in the form of hostile takeovers; external controls in the form of the role of the institutional shareholders, banks and competition; internal controls in the form of the existence of real independent directors on the boards, coupled with the existence of a ready market for managerial labor, act as tools to mitigate the governance problems arising in market-oriented governance models. The market for corporate control is supposedly the dominant disciplining mechanism to punish erring and under-performing managers.

Governance problems can be corrected by market threats of takeover if managers are found to be under-performing. Stock markets punish under-performing companies through low valuations. Companies that have low valuations are easy targets for takeovers. Acquirers vie for such companies, acquire them, sack the existing management and take all the present-value maximizing decisions, thus increasing the stock valuation. Fear of losing out to the market and fear of being sacked by the new management act as an incentive to the current management to take decisions aiming at improving shareholder value.

Similarly, the institutional investors and banks play a significant role in correcting the devious behavior of the mangers.[1] Since market-oriented companies are characterized by diffuse ownership structures and since institutional investors have higher stakes in corporations, they are motivated to threaten the incumbent management, of a management takeover in case of under-performance. Also by planting their representative in the board, institutional investors may coerce the executive to correct its value-eroding behavior. In extreme cases, the institutional investors and the banks may withdraw from their equity and debt-holding positions respectively and send signals to the stock market of the company's inability to perform well. This can reduce the valuation of the company's stocks in the markets.

Competition is a great leveler. Stiff competition from the industry might act as a check to the managers' self-value maximizing behavior. The greater the competition, the higher the motivation for the managers to disown slack and to demonstrate their superior performance against their competitors. Their dream to gain a better position in the managerial labor market and attract potential prospective corporations for their services, acts as a big mitigating factor to control governance problems in this governance model. Some empirical studies have contributed to the understanding that competition helps in stimulating the efforts put in by the managers and hence acts as a deterrent to pursuing individual self-serving goals. These incentives can take multiple forms such as higher monetary returns, market recognition, avenues for promotion, market estimate of the managers' current ability and future potential, managerial hubris of warding off competition, etc.

As per the recommendations of most corporate governance reports, fifty percent of the directors in any corporation must necessarily be independent directors. Corporations where boards are headed by non-executive chairmen must have at least one-third of the board strength as independent directors. These independent directors are to be deployed in the various recommended committees—audit committee, remuneration or compensation committee and nomination committee for transparency and fairness in the corporations' decision-making process.

Independent directors act as internal control mechanisms. They can either fire the managers or punish them appropriately on detecting misalignment of the mangers' interests with the shareholders'. The existence of truly independent directors acts as a big deterrent for the managers to pursue self-serving goals.

Most important of all, the existence of a ready managerial labor market helps in mitigating governance problems to a large extent.[2] A ready supply of competent and qualified managers in the managerial markets acts as a prod for the incumbent managers to perform well. Bad performers can be immediately replaced with the surfeit of talent available outside. Hence, the existence of managerial labor markets help in aligning the interests of the manager with that of the shareholder.

The United States and the United Kingdom are very typical examples of the market-centric governance model and have too many similarities to warrant a country-specific discussion.

RELATIONSHIP-ORIENTED MODEL

While the traditional corporate governance scholarship focused excessively on the after-effects of the separation of ownership from control, very little thought has been given to another competing governance dimension where ownership and control were either vested with a single equity holding entity or with a group of entities sharing relational ties. This was primarily due to the assumption made by researchers that Berle and Means firms existed worldwide.[3] While American corporations are characterized by diffusely held ownership structures, most continental and Asian countries are marked by concentrated ownership morphology. Traditional scholarship did not however account for this morphology. Thus even seven decades after Berle and Means proposed their theory of separation of ownership from control, research did not move away from its previous unilateral focus.

While the Anglo-Saxonic model of monist approach believes in creating value to the shareholder and hence is shareholder-centric, the Germano-Nippon corporations on the other hand, follow the pluralistic approach of corporate governance.[4] They recognize that entities other than the resource suppliers, hold a stake in the economic functioning of the corporations. Hence, central to their approach is the creation of value to each of these entities.

Since the firm enters into a nexus of contracts not only with the shareholder but also with a set of multiple actors, it is conditional upon the firm to distribute the value generated as a result of its operations, amongst all the actors.[5]

Characteristics of Relationship-based Governance Model

Relationship-based governance model is characterized by concentrated stock ownership, pyramidal structures and illiquid capital markets. Shareholders of corporations under such a model are driven by long-term commitment and are in a position to monitor managerial action. They thus avoid incurring agency costs. Banks dominate the shareholding composition by holding large amounts of equity. Also banks are directly involved in the operations of the firms in terms of monitoring, decision-making, etc. Unlike in the market-centric model where banks or the debt-holders withdraw from corporations in crunch situations, in the relationship-oriented model banks commit themselves to bailing out corporations that are having bad times.

Substantial cross ownership between firms is a characteristic feature of this model. Japanese keiretsu, Korean chaebol, French verrouillage along with the German model of relationship investing are glaring examples of the relationship-based model of governance.

As Cho and Kim through their study on the credit policies of Korea claim government-directed lending to industry has the benefit of subsidized and preferential loans as in the case of Korea. With more and more capital in hand, corporations are encouraged to expand their business. Hence, the few early corporations established within the relationship regime, have the incentive to diversify their business and grow as much as they desire. Capital is abundantly available to corporations due to benevolent governments at the helm. Corporations are largely left with the problem of mobilizing other operational resources that are required to keep them running.

In this governance model, the emphasis is more on cornering the maximum preferential treatment from the government. Two major parameters of the market-oriented model—capital requirements and control—are easily negotiated by the relationship-based model. While capital requirements are taken care of by the government-directed credit lending by banks and financial institutions, control too is not lost since the owners can manage to create a web of circular, interlocking shareholdings. Thus even with a minority share in the group company, the founder owners can control the corporation. By virtue of the cross-shareholdings, the minority shareholder can subterfuge the perceived ownership structure. There is enough international evidence to suggest that insider-oriented models are beset with the accumulation of control rights in excess of the cash flow rights.[6]

Companies that belong to a single group are known as *chaebols* in Korea and *kieretsus* in Japan. This ownership mirage led to the development of the majority-shareholder expropriating minority-shareholder hypothesis, whereas in reality, the so-perceived majority shareholder held minority shares.

This perceived concentration in ownership structures, reduces the owners' tolerance towards risk and hence governance is not confined to the market-driven demand of increasing short-term gains. The absence of such a discipline gives enough foothold to the founder-owner to circumvent risky and innovative business decisions. Indian corporate governance system too has been subject to such relationship governance, albeit, in a modified way.[7]

While France, Italy and Korea represent the relationship-oriented model, Japan and Germany have always stood for the entrenched relationships that existed between the government, industry and the other stakeholders. These two countries have provided two completely different versions of the relationship-based model and nevertheless proved that both are sustainable.

Primarily considered to be the most effective model of governance, despite being characterized by weak and illiquid capital markets, the relationship-oriented governance too is beset with many problems.

The dominance of banks in the decision-making process steals from the management its professional expertise and the corporation is run as per the whims and fancies of a few financial analysts. Excessive intrusion by the State in the corporations' affairs either through legislation or through its personnel, is a bane of the efficient functioning of the firm. For example, the State's control over French business, popularly known as *dirigisme* is imposed both directly and indirectly. Directly, State control is seen through its business interests in varied industries and indirectly, bureaucrats or retired public officials nominated by banks and financial institutions control private enterprises. Similarly, in Japan, the government plays an interventionist role with the Ministry of Finance maintaining strong regulatory control over business and supervising every aspect of industrial activity.

Since there is no or limited principal-agent relationship, what is observed mostly is the conflicts of interest amongst the multiple shareholders. While banks might want to get stable returns, the managers may be interested in personal growth, the suppliers may aim at getting sustained business orders and the affiliated companies might be looking for embryonic growth.

While some differences can be observed in the governance patterns of the relationship-based economies, the primary thread that unites all of them is the centrality of a web of relationships to run a corporation.[8] Hence a major factor that can be construed as a governance problem is that when one spoke of the relationship collapses and the other spokes fail to withstand the hub, the entire corporation is bound to collapse.

The German system of employee representation on the supervisory board and the Japanese system of employee promotion to board of directors helps keep a tab on the executive compensation. Hence, extracting of excessive rents by the managerial class is controlled fully.

Markets for corporate control are not as effective as disciplining mechanisms. Punitive measures like hostile takeovers are not necessary since management and the shareholders constantly interact with each other. Moreover, the direct involvement of all the constituent shareholders in some form or the other, in the operational activities of the corporation bars the choice of the managers to create information asymmetries. Fukao reasons that the core reason for the absence of a market for corporate control in relationship-oriented firms is due to the existence of implicit contractual agreements between the management and the various stakeholders. His point is validated given the general feeling amongst all stakeholders that the equity held by different shareholders is regarded more as a security for creditors than as a liability as is generally understood in the market-centric firms. Bolton and Von Thadden argue that the market for corporate control and ownership concentration are substitute mechanisms of corporate control. They posit that stock markets become active and liquid when ownership concentration is low and give rise to market control mechanisms like takeovers. Cross shareholdings help in warding off such threats of takeover.

Relationship-oriented firms being highly concentrated in nature are plagued by the attendant problems of non-specialization. Promoters double up as managers in most cases and if not, then excessive intrusion by the majority shareholders and the banks in the day-to-day operations may lead to corporate governance problems in the form of majority shareholder expropriating the value of the minority shareholders. Also, because of illiquid stock markets, risks do not spread out and chances of declining share prices may be high.

Some Examples

Japanese Corporate Governance—Keiretsu Model: Japanese governance system is typical of a relationship-based model of governance. Unlike the market-oriented model which emphasizes the importance of the shareholder and her value maximization, Japanese model seeks to balance amongst a wide range of shareholders such as managers, creditors, employees, partners and suppliers (Fukao, Ahmadjian). The

Japanese corporate governance system relies heavily on trust and relationship-based approach. Ownership is based on the *keiretsu* system (the Western equivalent of relationship investing), where the dominant shareholder is the main bank (or the *keiretsu* partner).[9] Banks hold a considerable chunk of ownership shares and fund the promoters whenever needed. Funding is not based on the notion of making short-term gains. Instead banks fund firms to build strong long-term relationships and play a very active role as big partners in the functioning of the firms. Japanese banks support their client firms by pumping in more capital at critical times. This, though, has eventually resulted in the banks accumulating higher non-performing loans. Sakuma states that during financial distress, banks take the control of firms. Only after there is some amount of recovery from distress and the firms start making profits, are they handed back to the incumbent management. Further the relationship can be defined to the extent that the bank not only provides equity but also places its executives in top management positions in firms where it has parked its finances.

Monks and Minow suggest that Japanese ownership system is interesting for in it cross shareholdings by affiliated companies, often including customers and suppliers, is found. Gedajlovic et al mention that investors like *antei kabunushi* or *seisaku toshika* meaning stable shareholders (such as banks, insurance companies and affiliated firms) have more than just an equity holding relationship with the firms they invest in. Both, Kester and Roe have argued that *seisaku toshikas* invest in relationship-building and growing business relationships rather than earning returns on their investments. Hence, interlocked cross-shareholdings are quite common in Japanese governance system and also equity is rarely diluted. Cross shareholdings have been instrumental in protecting against hostile takeovers.

The primary benefit of cross-shareholding pattern as Gerlach contends is that such close relationships amongst the various equity-holding groups helps in information sharing and thus promotes innovation, stability in employment and inter-firm cooperation.[10]

Rubach and Sebora suggest that neither the interests of the corporation nor the demands of the market seem to be more important than the conduct of the business for Japanese governance is characterized by life-time employment. The divergent equity-holders play a checks-and-balances role with their interdependent and mutual self-serving interests, leaving no space for opportunistic expropriation by one party of the other.

The government plays an interventionist role with the Ministry of Finance maintaining strong regulatory control over business and supervising every aspect of industrial activity. Retired government bureaucrats are placed on the boards of firms for effective management and to ensure effective implementation of government policies. Thus, Japanese relationship model is cast in a wide web of supports and balances. There are multiple monitors within the system as there are multiple supporters. However, as against the market-oriented governance system, the Japanese system provides no incentive to the shareholder to voice his/her dissent, for dividends are paid out at predetermined prices and hence any amount of noise made by pulling up lax corporate performance would not help. On the other hand, employees have the incentive to raise the standard of their productivity and help increase the profitability of the firms, which they may share as extra income, post-profitability.

Bankruptcy laws in Japan favor the creditors and hence corporate management loses absolute control to the banks. As Sakuma puts it, Japanese corporate governance is basically a contingent governance system with the main bank 'reigning in' the corporations whose financial conditions deteriorate. Hence the advantage of such a model is that an alternative governing body is always available and the basic purpose for which organizations work in Japan are served.[11]

German Corporate Governance—Co-deterministic Model: The German system of corporate governance is largely an insider-based model. Though ownership is shared by different groups of investors—banks, investment institutions, companies and government, yet banks control more of the corporate activities compared to the control exercised by the direct equity holders. German stock markets are relatively small and illiquid. Bank dominance coupled with weak capital markets further compels the German companies to resort to borrowings from banks giving much leeway for bank control. Also, banks draw their controlling power from the rights vested in them in the form of voting rights they possess because of their depositor-held shares.

Relationship between the banks and the corporations are so well entrenched that the banks have primarily emerged as key influencers of corporate governance practices in Germany. Banks' participation in business decisions by virtue of their lending, shareholding, voting and membership rights on supervisory boards, have led to a multiple relationship across layers of governance.

Unlike the unitary board structure prevalent in the market-based models, the German governance system is characterized by a two-tier board structure. German firms have a supervisory board (*aufsichtstrat*) and an executive or management board (*vorstand*).[12] The supervisory board has the shareholders, employees and unions as its members. The proportion of such members on the board is dependent on the specific type of company. While the management board takes all business decisions and for all practical reasons runs the company, the supervisory board's stamp of approval is mandatory for all actions. The supervisory board plays a critical role in disciplining the chief executive officer and approves the company's accounts, payment of dividends, appointment of management and also has a say in capital expenditures and strategic acquisitions of the company. The role thus played by employees through supervisory boards helps in attenuating private rent-seeking activities by managers or particular blockholders.

Voice given to the employees in German corporations mitigates a variety of costs that could otherwise be incurred, primarily, agency costs that are so characteristic of the market-oriented economies. Moreover, since compensation to members of the management board is determined by the supervisory board, expropriation through excessive self-remunerating instruments, unlike the Anglo-Saxonic model, is completely avoided.

Markets are virtually non-existent in Germany and hence market measures of discipline like the existence of markets for corporate control such as hostile takeovers, mergers and acquisition threat, and 'exit or voice' option of the small shareholder are not prevalent. This leads to weak corporate disclosures as per global requirements, but since banks are continuously in control over corporations, corporate mis-governance is to a large extent negated. Moreover, German system of governance draws its strength from the co-deterministic model where the supervisory and the management boards work in tandem to determine business policies and practices.

French Model: The French governance system is marked by the absence of a diverse investment community. The controlling interests in the French governance structure are held by the State, the banks and the corporate management, the State being the predominant player. To protect itself from unsolicited takeovers and strong competitors, the French business has developed a complex network of cross shareholding known as *verrouillage*. Under this system, shares are "parked" with friendly companies. Apart from cross shareholding, French companies are also characterized by interlocking boards. Interlocking boards hit at the roots of corporate governance by encouraging collusion amongst directors, harping on conflicts of interest and supporting information leakages.

The State's control over French business, popularly known as *dirigisme* is imposed both directly and indirectly. Directly, State control is seen through its business interests in varied industries and indirectly, one can observe the control it has over banks and financial institutions which lend capital to private enterprises, through its bureaucrats or retired public officials occupying prime positions.

SUMMARY

In this chapter, we have looked at the two prominently competing governance models. Each model has its own strengths and weaknesses. Scam after scam in the United States has shown the failure of the Anglo-Saxonic model, while at the same time one cannot deny the central role played by markets in bringing about a semblance of sanity to the way corporations are governed. The relationship-based model too is also under severe scrutiny in today's recessionary conditions. Which of them will emerge stronger to explain the nuances of corporate governance, is something that has to be seen once the ghost of recession is behind us.

DISCUSSION QUESTIONS

1. Explain the features of market-oriented governance model.
2. "Relationship-based governance model is a better model than market-oriented model". Do you agree?
3. Discuss keiretsu, co-determinism and verrouillage. How are they related?

NOTES

1. Refer to Short, M., (1994), "Ownership Control, Financial Structure and Performance of Firms", *Journal of Economic Surveys*, Vol. 8, No. 3, pp. 203–50 for a better understanding of the argument that control exerted by debt holders helps in influencing managerial behavior.
2. For a detailed understanding, refer to Fama, (1980), "Agency Problems and the Theory of the Firm", *Journal of Political Economy,* 88, 288–307.
3. Most empirical literature on the financial aspect of corporate governance was on US-based studies. Studies on corporate governance in

countries which were characterized by concentrated equity-holding corporations were conspicuously absent leading to the generalization of the Berle and Means' theory and its subsequent developments in the field of corporate governance.

4. Germano-Nippon: readers may please understand that all relationship-based models are classified under this terminology. For example economies like Korea, France, most East Asian countries and developing economies apart from Germany and Japan (as the classification indicates) which follow the relationship-oriented model are tabled under this classification. Germano-Nippon, much alike the Anglo-Saxonic model (which represents the market-oriented model) is common jargon in corporate governance literature. Germano-Nippon model is alternatively known as relationship-based model or insider-oriented governance model.
5. For a paper on value creation and value-sharing mechanisms, refer to Charreaux and Desbrieres, (2001), "Corporate Governance: Stake-holder Value versus Shareholder Value", Research Paper, Unversite de Bourgogne, France. This paper was originally published in French in *Finance Controle Strategie*, Vol. 1 No. 2, June (1988), pp. 57–88.
6. See Denis, K. Diane and J. John McConnell, (2003), "International Corporate Governance", *Journal of Financial and Quantitative Analysis*, Vol. 38, No. 1, pp. 1–36, for an interesting literature survey documenting the two generations of corporate governance research.
7. While relationship-based governance system helped the Indian industry to grow, market-oriented model has slowly set its foot in the governance model, what with the interest of foreign institutional investors in the Indian economy.
8. For a detailed study of the governance patterns in the different relationship-based economies refer to Monks, R.G and N. Minow, Corporate Governance, First edition, Blackwell Publishers, New York.
9. The Kieretsu is a complex pattern of cooperative and competitive relationships, characterized by shareholder interlocks (mochiai) and cross-holdings of debt and equity (Rubach and Sebora, 1998).
10. Non-sharing of information was precisely the problem that helped the Anglo-Saxonic model to grow.
11. Japanese governance unlike the Anglo-Saxonic governance model is not shareholder-centric. Instead, its focus is on stakeholder-benefits maximization and above all, providing lifetime employment to the employees.

12. All stock corporations Aktiengesellschaften (AG's) are required to have the two-tier structures. German limited liability companies, otherwise also known as GmbHs with less than 500 employees are, however, exempt from appointing supervisory boards. Employee representation on the supervisory boards could range from one-half to one-third of the board composition depending on whether the company is a 2000 employees plus corporation or has an employee strength between 500 and 2000.

Chapter 6

Transition and Growth Economies

TRANSITION ECONOMIES

While corporate governance has been a hotly debated policy topic in the Anglo-Saxonic economies for over three decades now, transition economies have woken up to this debate in the mid-1990s and are slowly coming to terms with international demands for better governance practices. Macroeconomic shocks and the State's inefficiency in managing corporate and industrial growth in transition economies has led to change in ownership from the State to private hands. How far this ownership transition has been successful is yet another matter for debate.

Central and Eastern European countries and the Newly Independent States (former Soviet Union) typically constitute the population of economies that have adopted the transition governance model. Interestingly, this form of governance model has been forcibly hoisted on their economic systems given their penchant to open their markets for capital requirements. Despite the difference in their institutional frameworks, there are many features which the transition countries share. They are characterized by weak, illiquid yet emerging stock markets; transition from a State-led enterprise to gradually seeping diffuse structures; transition in legal systems towards more competitive and functional systems; weak institutional set up to confront governance problems; poor investor protection mechanisms; lack of financial discipline; coercing the government into refinancing loss-making enterprises[1] and weak institutional investors.

Transition economies have undergone numerous structural changes after the State-owned enterprises opened up for private ownership. Only the ownership changed hands, yet in many cases, the State holds control over enterprises either directly or indirectly. In some countries like the Czech Republic, Poland, Russia and Hungary, mass voucher privatization programmes failed miserably. Mass privatization involved issuing vouchers to the managers and employees of transition companies at highly subsidized prices. Such vouchers in most cases could be exchanged for shares in companies. The basic premise on which the theory of mass privatization was based was the speedy transfer of ownership from the State to private entities. However, such voucher schemes failed to take off successfully owing to a wide dispersion of ownership which translated into ineffective monitoring of management.

In Hungary, the government had, in fact, to abandon the idea of voucher privatization. In what is known as 'spontaneous privatization,' managers of the erstwhile State firms managed to transfer their ownership from the State firms to the newly privatized firms at discounted share prices. The tunneling of assets by the majority shareholders and stripping the minority shareholders of their rights and value, have proved that the legal systems were ill equipped to foresee and mitigate such corporate disasters. Much like the market-centric and relationship-oriented firms, transition firms are also characterized by cross shareholding, both by individuals and enterprises. Foreign investment though eluded most of these countries with the exception of Estonia and Hungary, as transition economies feared the dominance of foreign ownership.

State intervention has taken a heavy toll on the transition model of governance. Economic inefficiencies are generated when the State imposes political objectives on the managers. Enterprises that have recently restructured themselves from State-owned enterprises to private ones, find it difficult to play to the tunes of the State but are helpless given that legislative powers are vested with the State. And to add to the excessive State intervention is the emergence of some powerful private players who by maintaining close ties with the government, obtain favorable finance for their projects. This phenomenon known as "crony capitalism" is a major deterrent for outside investors from investing in transition countries.

Despite their attempts, transition firms have been unsuccessful in emulating the market-centric model of diffuse ownership structures. Concentrated ownership can still be observed. Retail investors are few and far between. Liquidity of stocks is as good as nil with no or minimal retail participation. Hence the basic motivation with which the transition took place failed in the process of ownership transfer. Management initiative is stifled by the concentrated shareholders since they are in a position to directly monitor managerial performance.

The primary weakness of the transition model of governance is the lack of access to the external capital. Investors do not find transition systems convincing enough to pump funds. Initial insider bias that could be realized through privatization has weakened the financial system of the transition economies through misallocation and misappropriation of assets. External investors look for solid economic and legal systems that protect their investment interests. In the case of management failures, outside investors would like to gain control rights in the corporation through their stakes, which in a transition system is not possible given the artificial dispersion of shareholding. By artificial diffusion of ownership it is meant that though on the outside it may look like transition firms have moved from the concentrated State-led corporations to diffusely held privatized structures, yet in reality the web of cross shareholdings points to the contrary.

Individuals and companies hold a major chunk of the ownership pie through their networks.

In transition economies, neither the markets for corporate control nor the markets for managerial labor exist. Hence market control mechanisms like hostile takeovers, acquisitions and managerial punishment through ready markets for managerial labor, merely remain theories of academic interest.

Most transition economies have to come out of their conventional sectoral interests (like heavy industry, steel etc.) and enter newer sectors like services, if they are to fully embrace neo-governance mechanisms. Transition governance is a recent experiment with the governance adoption models. The outcome is to be seen once the dust of restructuring is settled. Whether markets succeed in correcting their governance problems or whether States bolster their financial and legal systems to keep in tune with the emerging governance needs, is a matter of speculation. Whether stock markets manage to meet international standards or whether they dwindle under the pressure of non-performance will be known in a few years from now. Whether majority shareholders still manage to expropriate minority shareholder value and strip them off their assets as was done during the early phases of the transition, or whether external investors manage to gain control rights and discipline the erring majority shareholders, remains a question to be answered by the transition governance mechanism.

Empirical studies on transitional economies have shown that countries that were characterized by high ownership concentration after the economic restructuring program have performed exceedingly well, financially.[2] Given this structure where countries are increasingly adopting market-models of governance but where insider systems are spawning good economic results, it is clear that since capital markets of the transition economies are not well developed, this dichotomy is set to prevail. However, efforts made by the transition countries to attract as much capital as possible to bolster their domestic economies has set a new trend of accepting and implementing global corporate best practices. Legislations to that effect are being made by some countries to make themselves attractive to foreign investors. Countries that have a strong legal system in place assuring investor protection and that have some mandated corporate governance systems are high on the list of foreign institutional investors.

Transition attempts from centrally planned economies to market decisive models would succeed only when corporations truly rely on the market power for their functioning. With little or no retail and institutional investors in transition firms, the transition model is hard pressed to rethink its economic strategies.

Of late, researchers are shedding their Anglo-Saxonic bias to understand the nuances of corporate governance in economies that are not characterized by the established models of governance. However, research in transition economies is easier said than done. Accurate data on ownership structures and firm performance are difficult to obtain due to a lack of historical data banks. Moreover, with the transition firms yet to come out of their transition blues, managers of such firms are less forthcoming in divulging any firm specific information which they fear could land in the hands of competitors or government authorities.

Some Examples

Hungary: Hungary is by far the most successful example of a transition economy. Hungarian industry, though, was not completely State-owned before the reform process. While most large enterprises were owned and controlled by the State, smaller firms were left to private ownership. The reform process has helped accelerate the change of ownership from the State to private players. Within a decade of the reform process, private Hungarian enterprises have begun contributing to over 80% of Hungary's GDP, up from 20% of their contribution in the pre-reform era.

Unlike other transition economies, Hungary had abandoned the idea of voucher privatization though it was mooted early on during the reform process. Instead 'spontaneous privatization' had become commonplace with managers transferring ownership of firms from the State to private companies. Under this programme, managers and employees were entitled to procure shares of the transitioned company at a discount of five to ten percent. However, surprisingly the managers and employees failed to muster controlling stakes in any company.

Kaminski and Ribound explain that a very clever strategy adopted by the State in selling off firms on a case-by-case basis to foreign investors led to an income of about $6.4 billion in foreign exchange for the State. This also meant that foreign investors ended up becoming the biggest stakeholders in Hungarian corporations, followed by other Hungarian corporate bodies which held cross shareholding stakes.

Slovenia: Slovenia is one of the breakaway countries of former Yugoslavia. Along with other transition economies, the new country has quickly adopted the transition model of governance.

In the pre-transition era, enterprises were socially owned and not State-owned. Social ownership relates to self-management contracts with the firms being run by managers and controlled by workers' councils (boards). In the wake of transition, social-owned enterprises were up for privatization with the rider that shares be allocated to a multitude of predefined allottees like employees, former employees, public/State funds and retail shareholders.[3] This meant that ownership assumed a dual character with a high degree of ownership concentration in the hands of institutional owners, alongside relatively small and diffused small shareholders.

In 1993, Slovenia adopted a new corporation law and fashioned itself on the German system of governance with a two-tier board system—supervisory board and management board. The supervisory board is mandated to have a minimum of three members. If the strength of the company is less than 1000 members, one-third of the supervisory board members are to be employee representatives. In cases where the employee strength is more than 1000, such representation is to be one-half of the strength of the supervisory board. While the employee representatives are elected by the employee councils, the members of the supervisory board are elected by the shareholders. Supervisory boards play a monitoring role and perform oversight and review duties. Management boards, on the other hand, are responsible for the executive management of the Slovenian firms. They run the day-to-day operations of the firms and provide regular reports to the supervisory board. Members of the management boards can be hired and fired and their compensation fixed by the supervisory boards.

Russia: A great deal of economic and political lessons were learnt by Russia with the collapse of the erstwhile USSR. To sustain itself in a fairly globalized world, inward looking politico-economic strategies had to be shed. Russia joined the bandwagon of transition to avoid getting caught in the web of economic despondency. From being an economy that fashioned itself on socialistic ideology by depending on its natural resources, Russia had to quickly move to embrace the socio-economic tenet of market capitalism.

The Russian model of privatization involved mass corporatization of State-owned enterprises. Employees and managers of such enterprises were given preferential treatment by transferring about 60% shares to them through voucherization programmes. Russian citizens too were sold shares of the transition firms through voucher schemes. Such vouchers were transferable in nature and about one-third of them were sold off by the citizens to foreign investors, thus allowing for a shake-up of the ownership structure of the transition firms. The government's objective of achieving dispersion of ownership among the Russian citizens failed with over 70% of the enterprises being owned by enterprise managers. Thus, ownership and control still largely rests with insiders.

Though it has initiated privatization, the government has not given away its ownership and control in many important sectors of the economy. Capital markets too are undeveloped and just about 20% of corporate shares are listed and tradable. Firms are asked to fund their needs through internal financing schemes or through profit repatriation.

Till about a decade back, the board of directors was considered unnecessary. However, with the growing exposure of the Russian economy to the global corporate governance models, Russia has recognized the need for establishing boards and actively encourages the separation of CEO and Chairman roles. Most Russian boards though are comprised of insiders, given their large shareholdings.

Ukraine: Ukraine is one amongst the newly independent States that have broken away from the erstwhile USSR. In 1992, Ukraine initiated its privatization programme with the aim of ensuring dispersed ownership of State-owned enterprises. As a consequence of this programme, enterprise insiders ended up garnering a major chunk of shares in many transition firms. The privatization programme was not adequately supported by institutional infrastructure. Stock exchanges were few and far between. Institutional protection to minority shareholders and investors was close to nil and the legal system was far from being developed. Despite the transition of State-owned enterprises into private hands, very few companies were listed on the stock exchanges.

However, over the last decade it has been observed that joint stock companies are booming in Ukraine, creating a need for effective regulation. The Ukraninan State Commission on Securities and Stock Market has of late realized the need to reckon international governance best practices and has regulations and rulings that establish shareholder rights strongly. How far and how quick Ukraine would be able to break free from the tag of being a follower of the transition governance model remains to be seen in the near future.

GROWTH ECONOMIES

An upcoming governance model, the growing economy model has not been documented separately in governance literature, as yet. Unlike the transition governance model which is an experiment to assimilate the bests of the market-centric and relationship-based models, the growth governance model is a fairly successful attempt in replicating the governance models of successful economies. Characterized by the existence of fairly vibrant capital markets; successful transition from State-held specialty sectors to widely-held firms; existence of relationship-based models as well as market-centric governance mechanisms; existence of an emerging managerial labor class; formal and functional legal systems; existence of both family-held firms as well as widely dispersed firms, the growth model of governance is a unique experiment amidst the much established Anglo-Saxonic and Germano-Nippon models.

Business groups dominate the growth economies with families retaining significant amount of control and ownership. Families with ancestral property that have entered the business scene some decades ago have now established themselves as frontrunners in the national economic systems. With the accrual of increasing profits, families that have started businesses in one industry have diversified and entered other industries and have gradually amassed a number of publicly traded firms to their credit. Interestingly, these business groups primarily managed and held by the families have modeled their control pattern on the relationship-based model. Also, quite interestingly, such firms have also embraced the market models of governance by listing themselves on the vibrant stock exchanges.

The growth economies have enabled a paradigmatic shift in the understanding of corporate governance mechanisms. While cross shareholding coupled with concentrated and pyramidal ownership structures is one feature of the model, another characteristic feature that sets it apart from the other models is the coexistence of fairly vibrant stock markets and the existence of the market for corporate control. India is a very good example of growth model of governance.

It is observed that families are no more dependent on their age-old talent to run corporations. Instead, the next generation family control is safely in the hands of qualified, competent and professional scions of the business family. Despite hiring professional managers to run the tactical operations of the firms, group firms do not panic about the managerial expropriation of shareholder value. Concentrated ownership structures give the families the much-needed monitoring control over the managers, as well as their professionalism disallows them to stifle management initiative.

The existence of business groups though has its own attendant problems. Conflicts of interest between the families and the minority shareholders erupt and the probability of the majority shareholder expropriating minority shareholders' value is high. Also problems in terms of transfer pricing; asset stealing; passing the profits made by one group firm to its sister firms; lending investment capital to other group members; profits shown by sales made internally and such other related malpractices, are likely to arise in such a setting.

Government-held banks that hold an ownership position in corporations are the major culprits of inaction and laxity. Whereas in the United States and the United Kingdom, institutional investors act as disciplining tools and are strong advocates of better governance practices, in the growth economies they are beset with problems of their own internal adjustments to the changing economic scenario. Institutional shareholding in growth economies is still in a nascent stage and hence, taking a strong position on the governance practices adopted by family-controlled corporations is a difficult task. However, of late, in some growth economies, institutional investors have begun actively participating in disciplining programmes that have thoroughly improved corporate governance practices.

The best feature of the growth model is the increasing realization by the State of its role in the governance process. While, on the one hand, the State has come out of many industries that were previously reserved for State control, giving way to privatized parties to take over, on the other hand, continuous improvisation in the legislations by bringing in amendments has strengthened the corporate governance system. Much like in the Anglo-Saxonic model, the growth economies augment the market regulators' powers to check corporate anomalies. How far market regulators have been able to use such powers to harness corporate mis-governance is yet to be seen. Political intervention stifling the regulators' initiative is widely rampant in such a model.

Markets for corporate control are gradually emerging in the growth economies.[4] Also market-disciplining mechanisms are found to be widely accepted in the corporate scene. Incidents of takeover threats and acquisition bids show that the growth economies have amalgamated in them the best of the market-centric and the relationship-based models of governance. Unlike the transition economies that are stuck with adjustments, growth economies have structurally adjusted themselves to develop new models of governance.

As of now, given the collapse of the market-oriented model in the face of bad corporate governance practices, the growth model of governance is demonstrating ample promise and is likely to stay. However, what remains to be fully demonstrated in the growth models is their ability to translate the existent systems into practically feasible governance mechanisms. A high degree of coherence between the government and the market regulator; the market regulator and the economic institutions; the government and the financial institutions; the legal systems and the capital markets—all these have to be clearly demonstrated if this model is to sustain itself like the market-oriented and relationship-based governance models.

Some Examples

China: China's industrial sector was dominated by State-owned enterprises till the late 1980s. There were no stock markets and hence no publicly listed companies. In 1990 and 1991, China established two national stock exchanges—Shanghai Stock Exchange (SHSE) and Shenzhen Stock Exchange.

China has over the past one decade made concerted efforts to bring about reforms in corporate governance. State-owned enterprises have been restructured, and foremost amongst the reforms, priorities have been accorded to developing capital markets and bringing about institutional changes to foster economic growth.

Public companies in China are characterized by a diverse set of shareholders—government, institutions, employees, foreign investors and retail shareholders. Government shares are held by the central or the local governments, or by government-owned enterprises. Institutions refer to domestic non-banking financial institutions like mutual funds, investment companies and trusts. Workers and managers comprise the employee shareholders.

Public listed firms have dual boards—the board of directors and the supervisory board. Boards comprise representatives from the State, legal-person shareholders, the largest shareholders and management. Retail representation is very minimal, though there is a provision for the representative of the public shareholders to be a member of the board of directors. Supervisory boards, on the other hand, have member representatives from the State, legal-person shareholder and employees, with the employee group forming a large chunk of the committee.

Usually boards consist of anywhere between five and nineteen directors, with about two-thirds of them being executive directors. Independent directors are few and far between and are a minority in the boards. The boards are responsible for (i) providing broader direction to the executive management, (ii) making strategic decisions relating to mergers and acquisitions, (iii) laying out company's investment, and (iv) financing plans and executing all resolutions passed by the shareholders.

The supervisory board, on the other hand, performs a watchdog function by (i) monitoring the board behavior and board meetings, (ii) keeping the shareholders' interests in mind and correcting any value-minimizing decisions taken by the boards, and (iii) keeping a tab on the financial operations of the company.

China's corporate governance regulations are, however, not very effective in protecting shareholder interests. Stock markets are driven more by speculation than respect for fundamentals. China Securities Regulatory Commission (CSRC) advocates some important corporate governance norms but conformity by the companies is rare.

Taiwan: One of the first economies to have led the East Asian Financial crisis in 1997, listed companies in Taiwan experienced financial collapse because of their controlling shareholders. Value stripping of the existing firms for the sake of assuming control was a common phenomenon during the pre-crisis period. Controlling shareholders played a big game in stock markets and subsequently set up smaller firms or subsidiaries which would then buy back the shares of the parent company from the stock markets, thus helping the controlling shareholder assume total control over the corporation. Existing stock would be pledged with the financial institutions and monies so obtained would be deployed to buy back shares of the parent company.

Taiwan's board structure is much like the German two-tier board system with the board of directors and the supervisory committee. This version is similar to that of the Chinese two-tier system with the board of directors assuming the broad directorial responsibilities and the supervisory committee playing the role of a monitor, watching the activities of the board. Representatives on both the board and the supervisory committee are elected by the shareholders and are shareholders themselves. A majority of the board representatives though are from the controlling group.

Argentina: Prior to 1991, Argentine corporate governance was much like that of India. Big business groups and family-owners dominated the ownership structure of a typical Argentine corporation. Businesses were funded either by the group companies or banks managed by the promoters or by State-owned banks. Founding families dominated the boards and outsiders were looked at with skepticism. Boards were subservient to the founder and hence had very limited role to play. A majority of the executive management were from the founding families and only a few outsiders who were loyal to the owners were appointed as managers. Very few companies were listed on the stock exchange as funds were not a major issue for the firms.

Post 1991, two major changes could be observed in the ownership structures of Argentine corporations. First, the ownership of State enterprises changed hands through privatization programmes. Second, a major restructuring could be achieved in traditional Argentine firms with families withdrawing from the "control" of firms paving the way for foreign groups and investment fund companies to gain both ownership and control.

Company financing too got redefined to a large extent with the acceptance of the importance of private placements and capital markets by the Argentine corporations. More and more firms are now resorting to private offers as a funding option and also, the stock markets in Argentina have become active in the recent times.

Brazil: Prior to the 1990s, Brazil's economy grew on import-substituting industrialization, with State playing a major role in promoting industry which was run by business groups. Family and State ownership and control was predominantly prevalent to the detriment of wealth erosion of a variety of stakeholders. Ownership was highly concentrated and even in the listed companies, ownership dispersion could not be observed. A majority of family firms had built up pyramidal structures to retain control. Moreover, these families also had their own banking ventures.

In 1991, Brazil liberalized its economy and opened it up to allow entry to multinational corporations. Also, as an after effect of liberalization, many State-owned industries were transferred to the private sector. Corporate ownership structures had to accommodate foreign investment and institutional investors like pension funds and investment banks. Of late, these new participants are playing a major role in improving the corporate governance of Brazilian enterprises.

Brazilian law makes provision for two kinds of boards—the actual board of directors known as "board of administration" and an audit committee known as the "fiscal board". While the board of administration is responsible for providing oversight and strategic direction to the management amongst other duties, the fiscal board is responsible for monitoring the firm's accounts and taking corrective action. The board of administration is completely controlled by the large shareholders—families and founders, loyal employees and connected political figures to be precise, and hence fail to perform stewardship duties in so far as protecting the interests of the minority shareholders is concerned.

Chile: Chile has been at the forefront of economic change for over three decades now. The first phase of privatizations happened during 1974–79 when State-owned firms were sold off to private groups thus allowing the spawning of new business groups. This was followed by a second phase of privatization during 1985–89 when State-owned banks and industrial enterprises were sold off to private players. Family-owned firms thus came into existence and over the time grew into significantly powerful business groups.

Chilean ownership structure may best be described as a highly concentrated one with the three largest shareholders owning over 75% of shares. Also, control can be seen vested with a few large shareholding groups through pyramidal structures created for this purpose.

Firm financing is largely done through internal accruals and inter-corporate loans. Also, most business groups own banks which act as instruments to tunnel investments to the parent firms. Banks have a short-term view of lending for investment purposes. However, what is interesting to note is the presence of institutional investors in the existing capital markets. They have been able to play a very important role in bringing about transparency in the corporate governance practices of Chilean enterprises.

Chile though has a very efficient regulatory system in place with tight frameworks for banks and financial institutions to conform to.

SUMMARY

In this chapter, we have touched upon two corporate governance models that are still in their nascence. Transition economies are still grappling with market-based realities and despite their supposed transition to market-based mechanisms, State's control of the corporations, directly or indirectly, is still seen. Growth economies, on the other hand, are trying to make the most of the best practices of the market-oriented and relationship-based models. While the business groups predominantly controlled by families bring in the relationship orientation, vibrant capital markets and ready availability of quality managerial labor characterize the market orientation of the growth model.

DISCUSSION QUESTIONS

1. What is meant by transition economy? Explain the chief characteristics of transition economies.
2. Which groups dominate the growth economy? Explain with examples.
3. Discuss the similarities in Argentinian and Brazilian governance models. How are they different from Ukranian and Hungarian governance models?

NOTES

1. Berglof, E. and E.V. Thadden, (1999) "The Changing Corporate Governance Paradigm: Implications for Transition and Developing Countries", William Davidson Institute, Working Paper Series No. 263.
2. For example, see Claessens, Djankov and Pohl, (1996) for studies on Czech Republic; Blasi and Shleifer (1996) for evidence on Russia; Frydman et al (1997) for a contradictarian evidence on the superior performance of State which is the largest owner after the post-privatization era in countries like the Czech Republic, Hungary and Poland.
3. See also Rado Bohinc and Stephen M Bainbridge, (1999), Corporate Governance in Post-Privatized Slovenia, Mimeo.
4. In the Indian case, the Bajoria-Bombay Dyeing episode has proved the existence of a strong market for corporate control.

Part IV

Miscellaneous

Chapter 7

Ethics and Social Responsibility

Business is a unique, complex and one of the most influential of all social institutions that has ever existed in human history. With the modern life dependent on business, every aspect of business like the products produced, quality offered, prices fixed and decisions made has a profound impact on societal dynamics.

Modern corporations are no more owned by single individuals. Separation of "control and from ownership" as maintained throughout the book has delegated the residual control rights i.e., decision-making rights to individuals managing the corporations. Managerial libertarianism has redefined the way corporations serve the interests of a variety of stakeholders. Modern theories of enterprise management are solidly ground in the perpetual dilemma of "conflicts of interest". Who is the manager supposed to serve? Who has the primary claims to the organization's resources? Why are there conflicts of interest at all? How should business conduct itself? What is the role of business in society? Is business morally or professionally obligated to serve the interests of a plethora of value claimants? How is business to structure itself in the ever-demanding, dynamic marketplace? Should the values of business be consistent with those of the society? Such questions throw ample light on why and how "ethics" is closely related to business.

Bad corporate governance practices like price fixing, industrial pollution, creating environmental imbalance, engaging in discriminatory practices, bribing government and bureaucrats for licenses, manipulating markets and stock behavior, indulging in insider trading practices have renewed the interest of the society and polity in pushing for adoption of ethical values in managing enterprises.

The capitalists' view is that the primary responsibility of business is to maximize shareholder wealth. Milton Friedman was an exponent of the shareholder theory, though he does not reject the responsibilities of individuals toward maximizing welfare of other constituents that are affected by business.[1] He argues, "There is one and only one social responsibility of business—to use its resources and engage in activities designed to increase its profits so long as it stays within the rules of the game, which is to say, engages in open and free competition without deception or fraud."

Corporation as a Social Institution

Modern business is strikingly different from its counterpart a century ago. Sweeping changes in size, organization structures, governmental regulations, capital needs and professional skills have marked the transformation of business from a slow-treading activity to a fast-paced economic institution. Developments in consumerist movements, growth of stake-claiming societies and the establishment of independent monitoring agencies by States have prodded the organizations to become more aware of themselves not only as economic institutions but also as active participants in the surrounding culture.

Modern-day corporations are looked upon as social institutions. They exist in societies and intend to serve them as well. As social institutions they provide an incentive structure to build the economy by maximizing the welfare of all stakeholding groups. Corporations are a center for agglomeration of individuals from the society who come together to serve their own interests in particular, as also the interests of the society in general. All activities of these individuals are mostly determined by social norms. As an institution, the primary function of business is the upkeep of the norms set out by society.

The role modern corporations play in society justify their claims of being social institutions. They provide employment to the labor in the society thus ensuring financial security to oneself and one's family. The needs of the consumers are catered to by the corporations in the form of goods and services. They provide opportunities for investors to make profits on their investments. By keeping the engines of business running they ensure that their suppliers do not run out of business. In short, they cater to most socio-economic needs. In the words of DesJardins and McCall, "from the perspective of society, however, the corporation is an institution that enables both human and material resources to be organized for the (one hopes) efficient production of the things the people of the society need to maintain a way of life."

Explained below are two different theories to explain the demand corporations implicitly face in their role as social institutions.

Social Contract Theory: As Jensen and Meckling state, the firm is a "*nexus of contracts*". Social contract theory has been hijacked from the realms of political philosophy to understand the functioning of modern day corporations. By "*social contract*" the political philosophers meant that the members of the society were bound by an implicit contract to enter into a civil set-up. This contract paved the way for legitimizing the rule of particular forms of government and also categorized explicitly the roles, duties and obligations of the rulers and the ruled. In a broader sense, individuals or parties to the contract promise each other to hand over their right to govern themselves by the sovereign.

In a similar vein, management thinkers have described the existence of a corporation in fulfillment of its social contract. It was assumed that the implicit contract binds the corporation to serve the society. Whether a particular contract is adequate or not depends on its acceptance or rejection by the parties to the contract.

The evolution of the modern corporation has altered the structural setting of the initial contract. In keeping with the demands of time, corporate behavior has changed which has had both desirable and undesirable consequences on the parties to the contract. For a corporation to behave responsibly in its dealings with multicultured stakeholders, each with its own line of thinking and own set of expectations, the contract has become more of an obligation than a definitive duty it engendered earlier. Some social scientists argue that any culturally specific contract specifying economic rights and duties must allow individuals both the right of informed consent to the contract's terms and the right to exit from the contract. This theory directs one to investigate whether corporations run on implied contracts or whether it is a model that is of no practical value.

Stakeholder Theory: Recent business literature is replete with arguments of stakeholder theory, with each researcher advancing the importance of this theory in line with her field of research. Interestingly, all arguments converge at a single hypothesis that business has to acknowledge the existence of a cross-section of parties (including the shareholders) be they individuals or groups—who benefit from or are harmed by—whose rights are violated or respected by corporate actions.

The stakeholder theory widens the base of a corporation's accountability and its responsibility, by citing different stakeholding parties to its activities. It encourages management to come out of the restricted box of shareholder theory and prods it to expand its consideration to include a concern for consumers, employees, suppliers, members of the community at large and all those constituents who are either directly or indirectly affected by its decisions. Please recall our discussion under *Shareholder-Stakeholder Debate* in Chapter 2.

Stakeholder theory recognizes that many constituencies affect corporate decision-making. Werhane and Freeman contend that stakeholder theory reckons plurality of values and moral agency at different levels and hence lays a good foundation for business ethics.

Every stakeholder is aligned with the corporation, either voluntarily or forcibly, to pursue his/her own interests. The more the stakeholding groups, the more is the complexity in catering to the needs of each party. The differing agendas leads to conflicts of interest not only amongst the stakeholders, but also between the management and the parties involved. Managers will either have to carve efficient strategies to do the balancing act where the interests of all parties are marginally met or simply dump the interests of some stakeholding groups in favor of some other parties depending on where the interests of the company lies. However, in cases of multiple conflicts, managers have the opportunity to pursue their own agenda of expropriating value in the form of rents like excess compensation, pay hikes, company sponsored sabbaticals etc.

Stakeholder theory is being professed vigorously by both academicians and practitioners alike, because of its inherent merits. It is all-inclusive in nature and takes into consideration all those parties who are affected by corporate actions.

Corporate Social Responsibility

For over five decades now, beginning with Howard Bowen's book titled *Social Responsibilities of the Businessman,* corporate social responsibility has been a hotly debated topic. As corporate governance literature gained prominence, corporate social responsibility got gradually entwined with it and has gained more visibility than ever.

Now corporate governance and corporate social responsibility are inseparable. Corporate governance is considered the vehicle to push managers into accepting broad ethical concerns during decision making. Corporate social responsibility "mirrors the company's conscience and long term commitment to stakeholder accountability".[2]

Corporate social responsibility is nothing but an ethical philosophy adopted by corporations to maximize the welfare of the society in which they operate. Business and society cannot work at cross purposes. They have to work together for the maximum good. Business organizations should not relegate themselves to just economic services but must realize that they are obligated to fulfill certain expectations that society has from business. Organizations need to keep in mind that apart from economic returns that they are to generate for the shareholders, they have to address social, legal, and environmental issues too. Social issues can range from taking care of the welfare needs of existing employees to providing employment to people from certain communities and localities, to ensuring recreational facilities of the society, to establishing educational institutions, to anything that is tangibly beneficial to the society at large. The range and level of societal commitment would depend on the size of the company and the area in which it operates. For example, a company like TISCO would prefer providing a township ambience to its stakeholders by providing good roads, establishing schools and colleges, setting up play areas and parks and recreational centres, since it operates in a larger geographical area and also because it is committed to running its business for generations to come. Also, the company may follow an equal opportunity policy which does not discriminate between gender, disabilities, region and multiple other discriminatory things to provide employment. On the other hand, a small company like Aptech which operates out of buildings in multiple locations would prefer tying up with education NGOs and set up grants to fund the education of poor children. Also, it may provide computer education for free in government schools. By doing so, both companies are exhibiting social responsibility. The magnitude differs based on the financial and geographical size of the company.

The recent case of Satyam fraud has not only hurt the interests of the shareholders but also exhibited its hollowness in so far as its corporate social responsibility is concerned. Ethical values should be imbibed by corporations for them to be socially responsible. Business ethics is not just about right or wrong, but is a philosophy that comprises principles and standards that guide business behavior, especially socially responsible behavior.

A B Carroll in her paper "Three Dimensional Conceptual Model of Corporate Social Performance" suggested that corporate social responsibility comprises four basic responsibility principles: (i) economic responsibilities—business obligation to produce goods and services to serve the consumption needs of the society; (ii) legal responsibilities—conforming to the laws of the land while pursuing economic goals; (iii) ethical responsibilities—going beyond legal frameworks and codes in creating a wholesome atmosphere for the society by not engaging in discriminatory practices, by not transferring social costs of running business to the society; by not engaging in unethical and immoral business practices; and (iv) discretionary responsibilities—engaging in philanthropic activities and other such value maximizing activities that are difficult to quantify and against any tangible measures.[3]

Corporate social responsibility literature has drawn extensively from subjects like economics, law and philosophy to explain the economic rationale of business behavior. This book limits itself to the evaluation of corporate social responsiveness of corporations in the light of ethical values practices by business. It is commonly understood that modern ethical theories can, to a large extent, form the basis on which responsible organizational decisions may be taken. Businesses can draw from extant ethical theories in designing their CSR practices thus bolstering their responsiveness to ethical dilemma resolutions.

Approaches to Ethical Decision Making

Managers have to take run-time business decisions and it is expected that they be governed by ethical norms while making such decisions. Sticking to ethical norms can be very difficult especially when business decisions are dependent on factors other than ethics. Assuming that businesses offer the managers enough scope in making ethical judgments, yet there are other factors like the organizational culture, shareholder values and societal norms etc. that govern ethical decision making. If sticking to ethical norms were a simple affair, we would not have dedicated a full chapter understanding the relevance of ethics to business.

Explained below are some important normative ethical models that help managers in making ethical business judgments.

Utilitarianism: The central philosophy underlying utilitarianism is directed at determining the moral worth of actions solely based on the consequences as a result of those actions. Utilitarianism seeks the greatest good for the greatest number. In other words, it tries to maximize the overall good or utility.

The utilitarian principle can be summarized in a single statement as follows: An action is right from an ethical point of view if and only if the sum total of utilities produced by the act is greater than the sum total of utilities produced by any other act the agent could have performed in its place (Velasquez).

The principle has been widely interpreted by the utilitarians in terms of what constitutes right action and what is meant by benefits. A right action is that which produces the most utility for all persons, agent inclusive, affected by the action. Amongst the many alternative actions, which may all seemingly look contentious, only that one action is considered right whose benefits outweigh the benefits that are accrued as a result of taking other actions. In taking such a right action one must consider the immediate and foreseeable future costs and benefits of that action as well as all the other contending actions. Such an action taken is bound to maximize value. But how does one determine the relative values of the consequences of a right action and the probable consequences of an action not taken? To remove these cobwebs, utilitarians distinguish between two types of values: intrinsic value and instrumental value. Intrinsic value is the good that is independently desired irrespective of any other benefits it produces. Any good that is valued for its own sake, which stands as a measurement metric for other goods, is supposed to have intrinsic values. On the other hand, goods that are considered valuable in so far as they lead to good consequences are known to have instrumental value. Hence actions that carry these values while maximizing overall good are considered to be the best actions.

Other Versions of Utilitarianism

Rule Utilitarianism: As Velasquez mentions, the import of rule utilitarianism can be summarized in the following two principles:

I. An action is right from an ethical point of view if and only if the action would be required by those moral rules that are correct.

II. A moral rule is correct if and only if the sum total of utilities produced if everyone were to follow that rule is greater than the sum total of utilities produced if everyone were to follow some alternative rule.

Rule utilitarians have shifted the focus from maximum utility to the analysis of moral rules. They contend that only those actions that are morally appropriate are right actions. If the benefits accrued out of an action that is followed by everyone (i.e., a morally correct rule) outweigh all the benefits that result out of an alternative rule, then the morally maximizing utility rule is the right rule.

However, it is commonly understood that utility can be maximized when rules provide for more exceptions. Exceptions to rules are exploited by self-interested individuals or the agents involved in the action to leave every one worse-off. Exceptions in rules are a must for achieving the objectives of maximizing overall good. In the process, exceptions breed benefactors in the form of individuals who are weak, self-centered, self-interested and who can stretch themselves to any extent to take advantages of the allowable exceptions.

Preference Utilitarianism: A more contemporary version of utilitarianism is preference utilitarianism. It advocates that human good lies in the satisfaction of one's wants or desires. Pursuit of one's wants should be valued for the inherent good it characterizes in terms of satisfaction if the want is fulfilled. Preference utilitarianists view that instead of ending up frustrated for not having satisfied one's wants, it is always better to take those actions that maximize satisfaction through want or desire fulfillment.

Interest Utilitarianism: An offshoot of preference utilitarianism, it rose in utilitarian theoretic arguments by criticizing the "theory of wants" of preference utilitarianism. Though not much different from the above arguments, interest utilitarianism emphasizes on "interests" instead of wants or desires. It advocates that a world in which people get as much of what is in their interests rather than as much as they want is ethically preferable.

Utilitarianism makes reference to character. It entails an ideal character, which is neither good nor rational to aim. Utilitarianism, on the whole, is found to be more idealistic than practical in nature.

Kantian Ethics: Quite contrary to the utilitarian view of taking only that right action that maximizes utility for all, Kant argues that only a "right" action needs to be taken because it is our moral duty to do so and not because of the consequences that it might beget later. He is of the opinion that the rightness or wrongness of an act does not depend on its effect or consequences. As long as the motive of the agent is good, it hardly matters whether happiness, perfection or agony results from the act. Acts do lead to some ends. The ends are immaterial if the act is done out of a moral obligation of duty. Kant lays down a fundamental principle known as categorical imperative: Always act so that you can will the maxim or determining principle of your action to become universal law; act so that you can will that everybody shall follow the principle of your action. The law is categorical because it provides for no exceptions and imperative because it is absolutely binding.

The import of categorical imperative lies in universalizing all moral acts that arise out of duty. No act, which is not obligated by duty, can be willed by individuals for universalization. That would ensure that posterity is served with only the right acts that are both moral and duty conscious.

Intertwined with the law of categorical imperative is another law: Act so as to treat humanity, whether in your own person or that of any other, in every case as an end in itself and never merely as a means. This law has a very serious implication for business actions, where individuals are used as a means to someone else's ends. If individuals are used as a means to produce goods and services, the law of categorical imperative holds good, since they are bound by duty to perform some acts despite their preferences. However, if they are exploited unlawfully as a means to some ends for which they are not obligated, then the act is considered immoral.

Rights Theory: One of the most important developments in ethical theories is the emergence of the theory of rights as an answer to moral obligations. Rights theory is generally categorized under three distinct headings: (i) human rights; (ii) legal rights; and (iii) moral rights. All the three categories overlap in the understanding of business practices from the rights theory perspective.

Rights theorists have proposed that rights and obligations have a cause–effect relationship. Obligations are derived from rights and rights best express the purpose of morality. Rights can be either positive or negative. Positive rights are implied obligations whereas negative rights are obligations demanded.

Virtue Theory: Virtue theory traces its roots to the ancient Greek philosophy of Socrates, Plato and Aristotle. Their focus on virtues i.e., traits of character as the subject of ethics, has found application in modern business theories. Virtue theorists lay much emphasis on the virtuous traits of individuals rather than on principles, rules, rights and obligations. They contend that a person with virtuous character would be motivated to act in ways that would lead to better consequences.

Virtues are to be acquired by people just like any other skills. Consistent practice and single-minded devotion to performing just acts makes a man just. Managers whose character is manifested by truthfulness, justice, compassion, respectfulness and patience exude positive energy to perform acts of benefits to the mankind. Agents who perform acts out of obligation exhibit no special moral character, whereas virtuous people are driven by the desire to perform all morally assertive acts, given the motivation ingrained in them by virtue of the traits they possess.

Value Theory: Value theory as a model seems to clearly establish a relation between normative and empirical business ethics. The most recent tenet for any modern corporation, if it is to survive in the dynamic market scenario, is that of maximization of stakeholder value.

Value is an adjectival connotation assigned to the consequences of a given act by individuals or groups, in conjunction with their needs and expectations from the act. Value depends on values and values are subject to individual sensibilities and hence are individualistically determined. The acceptance of certain values by an individual are not acts made at a contingent level; instead they come as a part of the mores of the society he/she lives in, the tradition he/she is an inheritor to. These mores have grown out of contextualistic, pragmatic practices.[4] Different mores ascribe different values to the same subject.

Values of individuals help in determining the value of an act–consequence. Under the stakeholder theory framework of business, different stakeholding parties have different value systems and each party imputes value to the act–consequence in line with its own accepted mores.

For the investor, value lies in the appreciation of the capital invested. The supplier looks at value as sustained business relationship with his client under acceptable profit margins. Value for the employee means job security coupled with acceptable pay. For the customer, value means good quality products and services at reasonable prices. Value for the society may lie in its overall development. Value mentioned above in each case is the most preliminary value ascribed by each stakeholding group to the act–consequence. However, each group may assign multiple value criterions to the same act–consequence. For example, for some employees the value of a job is its challenge or the satisfaction that it gives; for some, value may lie in liberty. Still for others, value means recognition. This may be referred to as secondary value.

In circumstances where there are multiple stakeholders, each with their pre-determined primary value connotation and subsequently, multiple secondary value determinations, the whole process of management becomes a complex, arduous affair. In the modern corporation where management is synonymous with the agent (or the manager) who too ascribes value to his/her employment both at primary and secondary levels, the stakes of delivering value to the stakeholders are too high. Of all resources that are employed by an organization, the managerial resource is the only and perhaps the most animate resource capable of employing, directing and extracting value from inanimate resources, both to serve itself and to meet the value determinations of parties internal and external (but holding some stake) to the organization.

Value theory integrates observational data with factual, empirical data to describe the existent relationships between various actors. Value theory assimilates as much data as possible on human behavior, its changes and its implications to the determination or discrimination of value. In doing so, it precisely understands human behavior because human-acts that are committed under some motivations affect all other parties related to the act. It investigates the claims of individuals of their rights to an assigned value by peeping into the gaps that exist between factuality and blind adherence to mores. Value theory goes about estimating value by first defining what value is and what its features are in a given case context.

Benefits of Corporate Social Responsibility

There are innumerable benefits for being socially responsible. By being proactively responsible industry can deflect formal regulation. In addition, ethical values adopted by a company get transferred to a multitude of stakeholders and in turn, they too are motivated to strive for the maximum good to the maximum people. Employee morale gets a big boost and they feel proud to be associated with a company that has adopted a culture of integrity as its basic business principle.

The company is reckoned as an epitome of integrity and hence its brand value and reputation soar northwards. Responsible behavior can itself be a source of competitive advantage.[5] There are lesser or no litigations against the company and non-business risks can be easily countenanced due to the company's socially responsible behavior. Legally too, a socially responsible company succeeds in complying with all the mandated regulations, thus avoiding itself the embarrassment of public scrutiny at a later stage. An added advantage of being socially responsible is that the legal and compliance costs are considerably lowered.

SUMMARY

Unethical business practices can bring in profits in the short run but cannot sustain corporations in the longer run. Businesses that reckon the rights of their stakeholders and deal with them in an ethical manner are always adored and continue to remain in business for decades and centuries.

This chapter dealt with the role that corporations are expected to play as social institutions and has directed the manager to draw from the extant ethical theories while making business decisions that are likely to impact a huge number of stakeholders. Likewise, it also lays emphasis on the importance of corporate social responsibility and the benefits that businesses can accrue by being socially responsible.

DISCUSSION QUESTIONS

1. "Corporations are social institutions". Do you agree with this statement?
2. Discuss social contract theory and stakeholder theory. What is common to both these theories?
3. Which ethical model in your opinion best explains ethical decision making and why?

NOTES

1. For a more detailed discussion, see Friedman, M., (1997), "The Social Responsibility of Business is to Increase Profits" in Beauchamp, L.T. and E.N. Bowie (ed) *Ethical Theory and Business*, Prentice-Hall, New Jersey, pp. 56–61.
2. Amiram Gill, (2008), "Corporate Governance as Social Responsibility", *Berkeley Journal of International Law*, Vol. 26, No. 2, pp. 452–78.
3. See Carroll, A. B., (1997), "Three Dimensional Conceptual Model of Corporate Social Performance", *Academy of Management Review*, Vol. 4, pp. 497–506.
4. By contextualistic, pragmatic practices, it is meant that society assigns some values to some acts not out of sheer foresight but depending on the necessity of the circumstances. However, these values hold good in the long-term either because they remain unchallenged or because of their implicit worth.
5. Porter, M.E and M.R. Kramer, (2006), "Strategy and Society: The Link Between Competitive Advantage and Corporate Social Responsibility", *Harvard Business Review*, Vol. 84, No. 12, pp. 78–92.

Chapter 8

REGULATION

Regulation has its roots in the Latin word "regula" meaning a rule. Regulation can mean the intervention of a public authority in controlling some unjustified action. Literature abounds with definitions of regulation. However such definitions are highly contextual and can mean different things in different settings.

Minogue defines regulation as "the use of public authority to set and apply rules and standards in an attempt to manipulate prices, quantities [and distribution] and quality of products".[1]

Within the context of corporate governance, regulation can mean intervention by the regulating authority—be it government, stock market regulator like SEC in the US and SEBI in India, or industry specific regulator like say IRDA for insurance industry, TRAI for telecommunications industry or CERC for electricity industry—to ensure that corporations take only such actions that maximize the benefits of all the stakeholders, without affecting the interests of any of them.

NEED FOR REGULATION

Why do we need regulation? The reader may recall an earlier discussion on the heterogeneity of individuals in the first chapter. Had all of us thought alike and behaved alike, there would be no conflicts at all and hence no need for regulation. But human behavior is capricious and dotted by different kinds of motivations. Corporations are no different as they are run by humans. In a bid to maximize their profits, they can severely hurt the interests of a few or many stakeholders. Regulation is indispensable to rein in such untoward behavior.

Under perfect market conditions, it is assumed that markets function at their maximum efficiency and hence cancel out any ill effects to the consumers. Markets are believed to be big levelers and regulations unnecessary. But in the real world, there is no such thing called perfect market competition. There are enough market distortions to warrant regulation, so that the end user of a company's or industry's products is not affected by the nonchalance displayed by the company or industry. Economic arguments too indicate at regulation as the necessary panacea to mitigate external market failures.

Becht et al in their book *Corporate Governance and Control* put forth two arguments for the need for regulation. First, they say, the owners at the time of conception of the enterprise may not be in a position to write efficient rules as they cannot foresee ex-post behavior of the firm and its actors, properly. Second, even if the owner has designed some rules ex-ante, he/she might want to break them as the composition of the enterprise changes. In both the cases, interests of certain stakeholders could get hurt. It is, therefore, important that there be some kind of regulatory intervention to circumvent such problems.

Governments regulate to ensure that the gap that exists between the producer and the consumer or the company and its stakeholders is narrowed. By themselves the consumers or the stakeholders might not be in a position to regulate the producer or the company as their options in their interaction with them is limited.

The reasons for regulation could be manifold such as excessive expropriation of stakeholder wealth by one or a group of stakeholders other than the one being affected, public outcry over protection of certain interests, industry excesses in terms of monopolizing product and services markets and failure of markets to punish deviants. Therefore regulation is needed to (i) build confidence in the minds of the stakeholders that their interests are being protected; (ii) mitigate financial mismanagement, (iii) ensure that companies deliver better and quality services to their stakeholders; (iv) control enterprises from expropriating stakeholder value; (v) ensure a fair rate of return to the investors and a better rate of satisfaction to the consumers; (vi) punish companies; and (vii) contain systemic risks that an industry gets exposed to.

Regulatory Context and Regulation Theories

Regulation is generally countenanced by those affected by it. Through regulation, resource redistribution is optimized in such ways that those who have higher stakes are given a bigger chunk of the resource and those with lesser stakes get a lesser share of the pie. When players with lesser stakes claim a larger share of the resource, either by exerting control gained by devious means or by maximizing gains from the existing lacunae in the market for regulation, government interference shapes up regulation.

Regulation as a pre-emptive mechanism is employed to ensure proper distribution of resources amongst a wider number of stakeholders. How effective has the regulation been and whether it was just, can be measured only post-regulation. Behavior of stakeholders on the allocation of a resource is gauged ex ante and steps are taken to regulate improper distribution of such resources through regulation.

Literature is abounding with examples of the government's choice of regulation for certain industries. Regulation, however, need not necessarily be limited to government intervention to correct problems arising out of market imperfections or natural monopolies.[2] Regulation can take shape either informally or explicitly. The rudimentary fact that drives regulation is the lack of robust methods to capture information asymmetries. Uche opines that "the end point of all regulatory processes is the enshrinement of some code of conduct for the regulated activity".[3]

But who decides this code of conduct? If the economist were to decide, then economic efficiency would be the pillar on which regulation would depend. On the other hand, if a full-time politician were to decide, then either ideologies or social experiences coupled with public perception of good, would decide the fate of regulation. If politicians were to decide from economists' perspective, then economies would achieve Utopian status. Regulation cannot be arbitrarily decided by the politicians just because they wield power. Regulation follows demand and supply phenomenon like any other market theory. The equilibrium condition is determined depending on whether a certain regulation is an outcome of public's demand or whether the regulatees themselves wanted to be regulated.

An argument goes that regulation is basically an outcome of interest group bargains and that parties interested in drawing synergies from the regulation would push the governments to enforce such a regulation. Interest group capture theory is an offshoot of this argument and has contributed heavily to the regulation literature.

If actions of individuals or bodies could be determined perfectly, ex ante, then laws could have been designed effectively and courts could have raised liability outcomes with ease. Since actions cannot be pre-judged in full, a proactive body like a regulator is created that readily responds to contingent imperfections. There are a variety of arguments to decide upon the implementation of a certain regulation.[4] However, public interest theory, capture theory and the economic theory of regulation are the most debated theories in the regulation literature.

Public interest theory: Public interest theory stands on the premise: markets operate inefficiently and hence need regulation. Government regulation being costless, it makes sense to regulate inadvertent industries that expropriate public wealth.[5] Governments choose regulations that maximize the welfare of the larger public. The choice of regulation though comes as a result of the demand for regulation from the public.[6] Hence the term "public interest". Basically, public interest theory is no more than a plain economic application to a political interest. Some regulation theorists have defined it as concomitant with "public choice" theory.

Public interest theory is embedded in the argument of market ineffectiveness in controlling inequities. Proponents of this theory argue that since governments are benevolent in nature, general interest regulations are passed on demand to regulate inequities. This theory has drawn a lot of flak due to its inherent weakness in arguments.[7] Posner argues that if the theory were correct, regulation would have been found to be mainly imposed on monopolies, which is usually not the case.[8]

Posner opines that no linkage could be evidenced in public interest literature on how public choice or perception of public interest gets translated into legislative action. Whether public, in unison, demand for a certain regulation and whether the demand is agreed to in toto is difficult to gauge. Is the public that demands a certain legislation the only voice of the population affected by some current act? Or are interest groups opinions passed off as public interest demands? Evidence found in theories like that of "free rider theory", which is very commonly used in finance literature, that all groups affected by some malicious act do not react equivocally clarifies that some people are not as much affected as others and hence the demand of the highly affected people might not necessarily be the demand of the mildly affected people. Therefore, the concept of majority demand in the framing of legislation defeats the purpose of regulation when some parties are affected in the bargain. Due to the uneven nature of the regulation, the regulatee might be in a position to exploit the weaker group.

Capture Theory: Capture theory is the precursor to economic theory of regulation. Unlike public interest theory, capture theory is more oriented towards reality. It argues that though regulation is introduced as a result of public demand for it, it is subsequently captured by the regulatee. The regulatee tries to draw synergies from the regulation and finds ways and means to translate the regulation into benefits. If the industry being regulated is big, industry cartels can be found to be formed to negotiate the impact of regulation to their possible advantages.

Modern economies are more and more inclining towards adopting Anglo-Saxonic forms. This breeds a class of capitalists who impact institution building to a very large extent. Also, capitalists make deliberate attempts to control these institutions. Regulatory bodies are no more than institutions and the attempts by the capitalists to play a dominating role over these bodies, tests the ability of government's effectiveness in framing these regulations as well as proves the vulnerability of such institutions.

Capture theory is the political scientists' version of regulation. They argue that regulatory agencies are not strong enough to withstand interest group pressures. Sooner or later they cave in and interest groups (regulatee industry cartels) overpower the agencies and dominate them to their advantage. The assumption of "capture theory" harps on the fact that regulatory agencies are inherently weak and do not have sufficient enforcement powers. The argument of weak enforcement can be found in the contention of Posner that there is a constant struggle for conquest by the regulatee on the regulator and that the regulatory process may be viewed as an outcome of informal or formal bargaining between the regulator and the regulatees. Regulation enforcement tends to become weak when a single regulator is empowered, though weakly, to regulate multiple industries. If the operations of all industries are homogeneous, regulation would be uniform. But since different industries operate under different conditions, affected by a variety of other laws, a uniform regulation process cannot hold good for all regulatees. This leads to the regulatees finding holes in the regulation content and regulation process that subsequently leads to industry cartels being formed that fight for domination over the agencies.[9] On the other hand, parties that are affected by these easy conquests of the regulatees demand for regulatory reform. Hence, agencies are always found wanting in terms of enforcement.

Another argument in the capture theory of regulation is that it is easy to subvert the regulator from regulating properly, since the key to all enforcements, i.e., information, is kept away from the regulating agencies. Regulatees hold all information and also reserve the ability to create information asymmetries to prevent themselves from being regulated. Howsoever strong the regulator might be, information asymmetries are bound to happen and the prime ingredient that is necessary for regulation reaches the regulator in a distorted manner. There is nothing a regulator can do about it despite the checks and balances that it creates for the regulatees. It is this power of creating information asymmetries that enables the regulatees to bargain with the regulating agencies. In due course of time, the regulatees capture the regulatory body and thereby the regulation.

Economic Theory of Regulation: Economic theory of regulation approaches the notion of regulation from an altogether different dimension. It takes us to the basic economic argument of demand and supply, and contends that regulation follows a demand and supply pattern and demand–supply curves follow regulator–regulatee diktats.[10] States supply regulation and interest groups demand regulation. The benefits accrued to the government or politicians against the supply of regulation could be in the form of votes or financial rents. On the other hand, the interest groups demand regulation for either tangible or intangible benefits. Tangible benefits could be in the form of seeking direct subsidies and controls on price-fixing. Intangible benefits could be in the form of thwarting potential entrants into the industry.

Kane casts the demand-supply notion of the economic theory of regulation in regulatory dialectic process.[11] The dialectic process may begin at any end—at the interest group level or the State level. Usually it is the interest groups that approach the State seeking regulations. This demand spurs the politicians to act and they gear up to supply regulations. Theoretically, the basis for supplying regulations should be the pre-assessment of post-regulation impact on the regulatees as well as on the contending stakeholding groups. However, much like the contract dilemma, regulations too cannot be framed fully for future behavioral moves by the different stakeholders cannot be pre-empted succinctly. Hence it is incumbent on the regulator to build in immunity into the regulation and the regulatory process, so that regulation deviance by the regulatees does not take place. Regulation deviance in turn would call for regulatory reforms and the cycle would continue.[12] Regulators that have been formed to play a pro-active role in monitoring malicious acts now would be no different than courts, should they engross themselves in tracking deviations, reforming regulatory processes and amending regulations.

Regulations like market entry control, price control, financial disclosures and monopolies restrictions help nurture the formation of industry cartels. Cartels thus formed either directly take up cudgels against the government or form an alliance with it to usurp control over regulation.[13] Regulators can be perceived to be effective if they were delegated adequate powers by the State. In case of State interference, regulation ends up as a rent generating mechanism. The regulatory body must be given enough control to act pro-actively in the interests of the protected group.

SELF-REGULATION

Originally drawn from the field psychological therapy, self-regulation has been extrapolated to organizational research first under the garb of self-management and then further expanding its scope to organizational regulation.[14]

Self-regulation refers to voluntary regulation by the regulatees without allowing for intervention by any public authority in regulating their activities. Many researchers have suggested that self-regulation is a government-initiated regulatory process which is transferred to the industry for implementation.[15]

Self-regulation, if properly implemented, eschews the need for formal regulatory mechanisms. Usually, professionals or industry bodies take the onus of formulating rules and procedures to contain self-serving behavior by firms. For e.g., Medical Council of India regulates the behavior of the doctors registered with it. This regulation is over and above the government-legislated regulation and could be in the form of punishing errant doctors or disaffiliating them from the council.

The biggest advantage of self-regulation is that it lowers the administrative costs of regulation in that the government's intervention is mostly avoided. Self-regulation is also advantageous for the individual firms as their costs of compliance come down considerably given the low-cost dispute resolution mechanisms. In reality, economic self-interests override voluntary regulation and hence despite the huge hue and cry over the need to self-regulate, very few industries or firms within industry sectors have successfully adopted self-regulation.

What is Good Regulation?

Good regulation is measured by two important parameters—quality of outcomes and the processes involved in regulating.

Quality of outcome may be measured against the effectiveness and efficiency of the regulation. Did the regulation achieve its welfare objectives set by the regulating authority? If the answer is no, then the regulation obviously is not an effective one. If the welfare objectives were met, then how efficient was the regulation? Efficiency can be measured in terms of costs—both administrative costs and compliance costs. Higher administrative costs can be a drain on the exchequer thus harming the interests of the common man. Likewise, higher compliance costs by the regulatees would mean higher costs to the consumers, as the regulatees are expected to pass on their costs to their customers.

Regulatory processes on the other hand, as Parker suggests, are measured by the balance that is achieved in terms of accountability, transparency and consistency by the regulating authority. Regulatory bodies need to be accountable for their actions and must function within the powers vested in them by law. They are not to arrive at decisions inadvertently. Instead, the established procedures should be followed before they condemn a firm for flouting a norm. The entire assessment system should be transparent so that there are no complaints from any stakeholders about the inappropriateness of the regulatory mechanism. Most importantly, the regulatory process should be consistent. Inconsistent processes do not evoke any confidence either in the regulatees or those that are affected by the regulatees' actions. Also, inconsistency in regulatory processes may raise administrative costs, thereby affecting those parties that are looking for justice.

Reasons for Regulatory Failure

The success of regulation is yet to be measured concretely. There are multiple opinions on the credibility of regulations. Market-oriented economies that are considered to be very tightly regulated do not give one the confidence to advocate regulation. For e.g., Enron crisis happened even while there were stringent regulations. In the aftermath of Enron, corporate governance norms were further tightened and regulatory bodies got more teeth than ever to contain such events. However, the recent sub-prime crisis in the US that has not only pushed many a bank towards bankruptcy but also jeopardized the country's economy has proved that regulation has not been effective. Relationship-oriented economies are not any better. While the East

Asian crisis in the late 1990s has exposed regulatory loopholes in these countries, the recent collapse of Japanese economy is testimony to the fact that regulations have never been better, else such crises would not have repetitively occurred.

Regulations fail due to multiple reasons, namely, (i) inadequately powered regulatory agencies; (ii) poor enforcement by the regulatory bodies; (iii) political intervention; (iv) inadequacy of human and technical resources; (v) high administrative costs of regulation; (vi) regulatory capture by regulatees; and (vii) poor regulation design.

SUMMARY

In this chapter, we have understood what regulation means and the need for regulation. It is common knowledge that regulation is needed to control actions that arise out of vested interests. Business is an agglomeration of stakeholders who in the process of working for their own interests create value for others. There are as many interests as there are stakeholders. If each stakeholder were to pursue his/her own interest, then it is obvious that conflicts of interest would become a prominent feature in managing business. Regulation is important to ensure that value of some stakeholders is not appropriated by decisions taken by other stakeholders.

The chapter briefly touched upon the concept of self-regulation and also explained the reasons behind regulatory failure.

DISCUSSION QUESTIONS

1. Define regulation and discuss the need for it.
2. What are the different types of regulation theories? Which according to you best explains regulation?
3. "Self regulation is always better than imposed regulation". Do you agree?

4. Explain good regulation. Also discuss the reasons for the failure of regulation.

NOTES

1. Minogue, M., (2002), "Governance-based Analysis of Regulation, Centre on Regulation and Competition", Vol. 3, *Working Paper Series*, University of Manchester, UK.
2. In the early economics literature on regulation, market imperfections were considered to be the only reason for State intervention and regulation was always subject to the government's intervention. However, later studies have defocused from this excessive interest in market imperfection argument and observed that reasons other than this could also explain regulation theory.
3. Uche, U.C., (2001), "The Theory of Regulation: A Review Article", *Journal of Financial Regulation and Compliance*, Vol. 9, No. 1, pp. 67–80.
4. For an authoritative review on non-economic, political dimension to regulation theory, see Purcell, M., (2002), "The State, Regulation and Global Restructuring: Reasserting the Political in Political Economy", *Review of International Political Economy*, 9:2, 298–332.
5. As Posner, (1974) argues that while public interest theorists believe that government regulation is costless, the costlessness concept is not well defined. The premise of costless regulation stands nullified in the face of mediation costs that are incurred by the government to generate regulations. Subsequent theories seem to have incorporated this fact and hence public interest theory lost its importance in the richness of other wealthy arguments.
6. Classic cases could be environmental regulations that regulate the levels of pollution in cities. These regulations come up because of a general hue and cry by the public.
7. Spierings, (1990) argues, "Suppliers of regulation are governments or politicians. In exchange for regulation they receive financial resources or votes. Demanders of regulation are specific interest groups. By regulation they try to expand their economic position, for example when they seek direct subsidies or money, control of entrants, polices which affect the production of complements or substitutes or price fixing". For a more detailed argument see, Spierings, R. (1990), "Reflections on the Regulation of Financial Intermediaries", *KYKLOS*, Vol. 43, 1, 91–109.

8. Refer to Posner (1974) for an authoritative study on regulation, "Theories of Economic Regulation", *The Bell Journal of Economics and Management Science*, Vol. 5, 336.
9. Here I use the word 'agency' synonymously with 'regulatory body' and 'regulator'.
10. This theory has a critic in Posner who argues that the theory of economic regulation cannot be empirically tested since demand and supply curves in this context cannot be measured. In the regulatory process, demand and supply is basically a behavioral process which cannot be subject to quantification to gather empirical evidence. The benefits accrued to both the regulator and the regulatee are basically kept under wraps in fear of public criticism and the concomitant losses.
11. Kane, E.J. (1981), Impact of Regulation on Economic Behavior, *The Journal of Finance*, Vol. 36, pp. 355–67 and Kane, E.J. (1983), "Policy Implications of Structural Changes in Financial Markets", *American Economic Review*, Vol. 73, pp. 96–100.
12. The term "regulatory reforms" was introduced into regulation literature by Kay and Vickers (1988) in their seminal study, "Regulatory Reform in Britain", *Economic Policy*, Vol. 5, pp. 286–351.
13. Regulation theorists could not explain the degree of overlap that exists between the three theories of regulation.
14. See also Tsui, A.S. and S.J. Ashford, (1994) "Adaptive Self-regulation: A Process View of Managerial Effectiveness", *Journal of Management*, Vol. 20, No. 1, pp. 93–121. Also, read Kanfer, F.H. and P. Karoly, (1972) "Self-control: A behavioristic excursion into the lion's den, Behavior Therapy", 3: 398–416 for connect to the psychological therapy theory.
15. Asby et al. (2003), *Industry Self-Regulation: A Game Theoretic Typology of Strategic Voluntary Compliance*; Gupta, A.K. and L.J. Lad, (1983), Industry Self-Regulation: An Economic, Organizational and Political Analysis, *Academy of Management Review*, 8(3), pp. 416–425; Ogus, A.I. (1994) *Regulation: Legal Form and Economic Theory*, Oxford University Press; Baggot, R. (1989), "Regulatory Reform in Britain: The Changing Face of Self-Regulation", *Public Administration*, 67, 435–454.

Chapter 9

Divergence, not Convergence

The literature on corporate governance is largely based on the available governance variants and the comparative significance of one variant over the other. Most studies have followed the "mutually exclusive" norm to explain country-specific governance models by relating to either of the two popular variants—market-oriented model and relationship model. The globalization wave of 1990s has severely challenged the existing business practices the world over. Demand for better corporate governance in particular has ushered in a paradigm shift in the way businesses are conducted. While the United States and the United Kingdom provide an interesting market-oriented model to emulate, the relationship-oriented models also provide an alternative pattern for successful governance mechanisms. While some authors contend that countries that have adopted the Anglo–Saxonic market-oriented model have been successful in all aspects of business, others argue that the developed countries could afford to adopt the market models only after attaining a critical mass, through allowing for a considerable period of protective regime. Nevertheless, Germano-Nippon-based relationship-oriented model proves that capital markets are not the only institutions from where money can be raised. While capital markets provide ready access to funds, they also play a devil's role in pushing the managers for short-term gains which results in a host of corporate governance problems. On the other hand, relationship-oriented economies thrive on their connectedness and are supposedly not too harsh on managers which again lead to a host of corporate governance issues.

DEBATES ON DIVERGENCE

Many governance scholars foresee the convergence of corporate governance practices and have vehemently advocated the same. However, convergence cannot be achieved in totality unless countries follow a common corporate legal code.

Since countries differ in their political structures, similarity in governance processes is highly unlikely. Political institutions of a country define its economic models. Countries do model their governance patterns on the paths that they have inherited. However, recent attempts by some transition countries to emulate the governance practices of other countries have led to some interesting developments. New paradigms of corporate governance are emerging. Excessive inclination of transition economies to adopt market-centric models of governance has led to a lot of turbulence in these countries.

Corporate governance problems do not end by imitating best practices of some other country. Instead, concerted efforts by countries to understand their internal strengths—be they relationship-based governance processes, State-led economies or market-centric models—and develop a governance model unique to their needs would certainly bolster their corporate governance practices.

Convergence in corporate governance practices is certainly not possible given the existence of divergent legal and political systems prevailing in different countries. The current drift of some countries towards the outsider-oriented model is an economic fad and will correct itself once countries fail to adopt the market models fully. Nevertheless, newer paradigms of corporate governance practices will emerge in the experimental economies with the right balance of market-oriented, relationship-based and the native models of governance.

Two very important debates that have emerged to explain the reasons behind the divergent corporate governance laws across different countries are the theories of political preconditions and path dependency.

Political Preconditions Argument: Unlike the United States or other market-oriented economies that are characterized by diffuse ownership structures and therefore the tying of the managers' interests with the shareholders' interests become central to the corporate governance agenda, developing economies and insider-oriented nations are more motivated by the social welfare motives. In a very interesting paper titled "Political Foundations for Separating Ownership from Corporate Control", Roe argues that managers are compelled by the social democracies to forego some profit maximizing goals for public welfare, to ensure employment stabilization and to use capital to keep the business going at a stable rate instead of downsizing at times, when the markets are not aligned to the firm's production capabilities.

The very fabric of social democracy calls for the protection of employee interests whenever there is a conflict between the employees and the shareholders. This leads to an increase in agency costs in such countries provided control is in the hands of the managerial class. Given the underdeveloped capital markets scenario in such economies, the rising agency costs are far from being controlled by the market forces. Also, in such democracies, shareholder value added is less due to opaque accounting policies. Owners are neither necessarily motivated nor compelled to reveal accounting and remuneration information to their employees for fear of employee reprisal in the form of demands for better security and wages. Social democracies in one way help in the private extraction of benefits by the owners that is otherwise not possible in market-oriented systems of governance.

Hence, given the differences in the political perspectives of nations, it is difficult for any nation to quickly adapt to foreign best practices. Some economies are in better position to agglomerate capital due to their political presence internationally and also because their internal structures of governance are so well defined that spreading risk becomes easier for them. Liquid capital markets coupled with strong institutional investors design and redefine corporate best practices through their monitoring and control roles. Only when political governance mandates such a structure of market dependence, can businesses be held directly accountable to the investors.

On the other hand, countries that are plagued with opportunistic political interests fail to emerge as powerful drivers of change. Domestic political bickering, corruption, nepotism coupled with protectionism hinder progress in mandating laws that are consistent with international corporate governance needs. However, it should not be construed that economies that do not adopt international forms or norms relegate themselves to economic backwardness. Though countries like Japan, Korea and Germany do not have highly active capital markets and are burdened with union problems and/ or employee security and welfare problems, yet their corporate governance practices are comparably amongst the best in the world.

One cannot conclusively say that a given form of political structure would lead to better corporate governance results. Where the United States and the United Kingdom are performing with their market-centric models, Germany, Japan and France too are performing equally well with their insider models of governance. What is thus more important are the political preconditions that compel the governance practices of corporations. Social democracies might have strong legal systems that protect employee interests whereas market-dominated capitalistic economies might have strong investor protection mechanisms. This divergence in the legal systems of nations thus leads to the divergence in corporate governance practices.

Path Dependence Argument: The primary contribution to the development of this argument was made by Lucian Bebchuk and Mark Roe in their seminal paper "A theory of path dependence in corporate ownership and governance". Later studies have either concurred with or advanced their arguments.

The theory of path dependence highlights the reasons on why despite international pressures to converge, some economies vary in their governance processes. Though business practices are seen converging in the advanced economies, individual nations are not concomitantly exerting their efforts to converge their legal and economic systems with international changes. Bebchuk and Roe argue that this is typical of a path-dependent phenomenon that is driven either by structure or rule-dependent mechanisms governing a country. By structure-driven path dependency, they mean that any subsequent ownership structures in a given economy is largely a result of the "initial" ownership conditions and structures of the economy. Rule-driven path dependency relates to the impact the initial ownership structures have on the subsequent ownership structures through their effect on the nation's corporate laws.

The rent-seeking behavior of the controlling owners would thwart all efforts in rationalizing legal systems that would call for or encourage the emergence of financial institutions to accumulate and hold large blocks of shares. When the private benefits of control are large, large blockholders would resist all means to garner extra capital from the markets because that would leave them with lesser control over the corporations they hold. However, it is argued, that though this behavior of controlling shareholders gets reflected at contingent levels, the roots to it lay in the initial ownership structures that started with the economy. The subsequent structures only fight to maintain the status quo to be able to extract private benefits of control.

There is less scope for either the ownership structures or the concomitant corporate control structures to converge on one single variant of governance. The difference in ownership structures still persists due to factors like sunk costs, complementarities, network externalities and endowment effects that have affected the initial ownership structures. Also reasons like persistence by the managers to extract rents from diffused ownership groups and the persistence of the controlling owners to extract private rents contribute towards non-convergence of ownership structures.

Rule-driven path dependence, on the other hand, suggests that though there may be convergence in the economic systems of any two nations, the rules that they follow might still differ due to initial rule patterns that individual nations adopted with their initial ownership structures. For example, though transition countries might privatize and become market-oriented in nature, the rules that they had followed in the pre-privatization era would still stick to their post-privatized control structures, making transition a difficult and painful process. Giving up initial rule patterns to adopt newer ones is not easy since legal rules are often by-products of political processes. While the initial corporate structures are established, the role of interest group politics to push governments for mandating rules in favor of their interests has a big impact on the emergence of subsequent corporate structures and rules governing these structures. The power that these existing patterns of ownership structures can exert, on the policy makers at later stages to maintain the status quo or to change the rules in ways conducive to their rent extraction benefits, affects the path dependence of a rule-driven governance structure.

Schmidt and Spindler forward two explanations for path dependence. The first, they argue, is that path dependence is a consequence of switching costs. While decisions which seemed appropriate at a time when they were taken might not hold good in subsequent periods, the high costs that are tied up to the previous decisions might render it difficult to switch to newer alternatives at times when the older decisions become inappropriate. Though inefficiencies in earlier arrangements are conspicuously observed, a switch-over decision cannot be effected due to the high costs involved. This forces one to stick to the path-dependent arrangement and accept inefficiencies.

The authors also suggest that path dependence is a consequence of evolutionary myopia. They argue that evolving systems respond to global pressure by attaining local optima. This is primarily because of the historicity of the system at that given point of time. This explanation assumes that local optima are achieved because actors taking decisions are under the presumption that under pressure they had adjusted their system through rational decisions. The decision makers, through their shortsightedness, are not able to take such decisions under pressure that would hold good in the long run. However, the decisions taken seem to meet contingent level problems in the highest possible rational way. This explanation thus contributes to the argument that the evolution of firms thus turns out to be path-dependent.

In his brilliant article, "Why are Institutions the Carriers of History? Path Dependence and the Evolution of Conventions, Organizations and Institutions", David provides three analytical explanations on why history matters to understand path dependence in economic phenomena.[1] In his words, "… the first has to do with the role of historical experience in the formation of structures of mutually consistent expectations that enable coordination to be achieved without centralized direction of the actions of individual economic agents. The second is concerned with the resemblance between the information channels and codes that multiperson organizations require in order to function with even a minimum viable level of efficiency and durable physical capital goods. The third involves the implications of strong complementarities, or interrelatedness—and the consequent necessity of achieving consistency and compatibility—among the constituent elements of complex human organizations".

Explaining the failure of Russian liberalization programme, Hedlund takes the argument back to the extant path-dependent structures that have bogged the programme. While Russia was inching towards reforms and adopting Western practices, under external shock to the economy, path-dependent structures have either rendered it impossible to move from the prevailing norm systems or have responded to the shocks for a short period only to gravitate back to the extant patterns. Policy improvisations did not mesh well with the prevailing social and economic conditions and hence the reform process turned out to be a total mess. This can further be substantiated by quoting McDaniel's work, that Russian ideology is grounded in binary absolutism. For the Russians there are only two options available. Under the "either is" argument, one is left with no viable rational decision-making option, with no room for compromise. This mental model has deprived the Russian attempt to break out of the economic inequilibrium, which Hedlund describes as the reversal of the system to its original institutional position.[2]

North observes that institutional change follows typical path-dependent models. Mental models have a lot to do in shaping human perception of the good and bad. What constitutes good institutions and what elements make a bad institution, depend on the beliefs that individuals have and hence any change would most necessarily be incremental in nature. Institutional changes do not happen all of a sudden. They follow the path-dependent incremental models for change.

Thus it is argued that though there is much speculation in favor of convergence of corporate governance practices, unless there is a convergence in the legal systems of nations, the likelihood of the former is rather remote.

Further Arguments for Non-convergence

The biggest challenges to global corporate governance is thus convergence of corporate best practices as well as convergence of global corporate legal systems. Political will is absolutely crucial to the developing of means and methods to integrate domestic corporate practices with the best standards followed internationally. Only then can integrity of a country's economic system get reflected properly and foreign investment in domestic business increase. Mere compilation of governance reports and recommendations to keep in tune with the developments across the globe would not ensure good governance practices. Given the voluntary nature of compliance to the recommendations, many economies, especially Asian nations that are inured to complete freedom and unbridled excesses, may not like to voluntarily disclose their business transactions. This, then, would leave a large gap in the country's business governance integrity.

Establishing legal systems to ensure the growth of institutional ownership is perhaps the biggest challenge facing global corporate governance today. In a situation where the dichotomy of outside-oriented insider-led systems is in place in most post-privatized transition economies, institution building remains a big challenge. Efforts towards developing liquid markets along with the systemic growth of institutional investors would help in adopting global standards of corporate best practices.

Achieving uniformity in board architecture across nations would be a difficult task. Though the recommendations of the need for a majority of independent directors on corporate boards is universally acclaimed, yet most countries practicing insider system of governance would stop short of adopting it. Independent directors may hinder the blockholders from engaging in rent-seeking activities. However, the practicality of having a majority of independent directors even in market-oriented models is questionable given the role of the chief executive officers in their nomination and appointment. Also, managerial expropriation of shareholder wealth may be hindered in their presence if they really set out on the task for which they were appointed.

Another important area of concern is the split in the roles of the chairman and the chief executive officer. The market-oriented models demand separate individuals for the two positions. Also the demand for a non-executive to act as the chairman of a corporation is made, some insider-oriented countries like France do not follow this practice and yet are highly successful. In France, the prevalent Societe Anonyme structure contains a president directeur-general (PDG) who runs both the board and the company. Similarly, in most Asian countries both the positions are held by the same person, most often, by the person holding a majority block in the company's shares.

Achieving complete compliance with the disclosure mandates would be a Herculean task. Corporations that are typical of the path-dependent structures may not be motivated to disclose their financial data as per the recommended norms for fear of both external and internal reprisals. If their accounting data is not in concomitance with the market expectations, then the markets might punish them by lowering their market value. On the other hand, if honest reporting of owner compensation and remuneration of executives were done, then employees might retaliate if a huge disparity in compensation structures is found. No family-controlled or even otherwise, closely-held businesses would thus be interested to disclose compensation-related information correctly. In such situations, where market-oriented models of governance call for open disclosures and insider models do not compel for such disclosures, convergence in corporate governance mechanisms seem to be too far to achieve.

Legal systems are sometimes more influenced by corporate lobbying. As mentioned in the path-dependent arguments, certain control structures enable the corporations to be in better negotiating positions vis-à-vis national regulatory bodies. Through their power to manipulate the legal mandates towards their private benefits, existent corporate structures might create roadblocks to the efforts made for adopting global best practices.

Much also depends on the political ideologies that nations follow. Cultural differences in national ideologies stand to hinder the convergence of corporate governance mechanisms. Where social democracies are characterized by their commitment to ameliorate public welfare, capitalistic economies, on the other hand, are focused towards enhancing shareholder value. Capitalistic virtues like profit maximization are considered vices in social democracies. Countries that are dictated by policies of life-long employment (e.g., Japan) and co-deterministic practices (e.g., Germany) adopt mechanisms other than market-oriented for fear of markets influencing and or determining national policies in the long run. Corporate cultures in the transition countries are newly emerging with states relinquishing control of business. The bureaucratic nature of State-led corporations was fatal in attracting investor attention. Post-privatization benefits can however be seen now with foreign investment in transition countries. These countries are in a stage of metamorphosis and most of them are fluctuating between the two extreme governance models. Employees and managers who worked for the State-led corporations have emerged as the neo-owners and given the time they would need to adapt themselves to the needs of international governance practices, convergence seems to be a distant dream.

SUMMARY

The challenges that confront the corporate governance process differ from country to country. Nations that have rationalized their corporate laws in concordance with international norms still have to search for better systems given the uncertainty in global governance advancements. On the other hand, countries that tend to accommodate paradigmatic governance shifts may tend to worsen off their performances. A prisoners' dilemma always exists on whether convergence would be ideal or divergence would maximize the value added.

DISCUSSION QUESTIONS

1. "Convergence in corporate governance models is impossible". Do you agree?
2. Explain the difference between political preconditions theory and path dependence.

NOTES

1. David, P.A., (1994), "Why are Institutions the Carriers of History? Path Dependence and the Evolution of Coventions, Organizations and Institutions", *Structural Change and Economic Dynamics*, Vol. 5, No. 2, pp. 205–20.
2. Refer to Hedlund, S., (2000), "Path Dependence in Russian Policy Making: Constraints on Putin's Economic Choice", *Post-Communist Economies*, Vol. 12, No. 4, pp. 389–407 for a study of Russian Path Dependence and an explanation of the concept of 'revealed institutional preference'.

Part V

Corporate Governance in India

Chapter 10

Systemic Development

While different authors have come up with different theories on the evolution of corporate governance in India, in this section you will be introduced to two popular period-based arguments. The chapters in this section attempt to unravel the mystery surrounding corporate governance scholarship in the context of the development of the concept in India. The chapter begins by highlighting the common and most widely-held belief of the development of corporate governance. However, through the ensuing debates in this chapter and the chapter following it, an attempt is made to rethink its emergence from two new perspectives—systemic perspective and relationship perspective. The two perspectives focus on understanding how corporate governance measures have ended up as by-products of economic liberalization, while corporate mis-governance was all the while prevalent, right through independence, and yet was ignored.

Systemic perspective refers to the internal changes in the control structures of the organizations, coupled with macro-economic changes that created space for mis-governance, while relationship perspective refers to the hand-in-glove relationship between the industry and the State that dented corporate governance. Both these arguments contain in them the seeds of a later-day corporate governance scholarship.

Common Conception of Emergence of CG in India

Before the onset of liberalization, the Indian organized sector was dominated by public enterprises and their performance was always found wanting. The performance of the private sector was also not up to the mark.[1] Both the public and the private sector enterprises had to brace up to meet the challenges of globalization. Moreover, with foreign investment in Indian industry, accountability to shareholders had become a necessity if one had to attract more capital to grow. Also with the institutional investors emulating the practices of their counterparts from the developed economies, better governance practices had to be adopted for such organizations to sustain themselves for longer periods.

The demands of financial liberalization have helped in imparting greater control to the banks in their operations.[2] This led to the banks extending external finance in lieu of some control rights. Since the structure of corporate finance in India is highly dependent on the banks' financial resources, some authors argue that legal structures should be so developed that banks are freed from excessive portfolio restrictions like priority sector lending, and governance mechanisms be so devised that bank representations on boards become a reality. This would enable banks to maintain proper checks and balances apropos of expropriation of shareholder value by the managers.

Varied opinions were articulated in India in response to wide-ranging corporate scandals like violation of foreign exchange regulations, making clandestine payments to politicians, involvement in illegal activities and shady deals by the top industrial houses.[3] While some suggested that the investigations might scare away the foreign investors and the economy would once again be in tatters, others placed stress on the importance of social responsibilities of business. However, not until the groundwork done in terms of preparing a code for corporate conduct by the Confederation of Indian Industries (CII) in 1998, was the importance of corporate governance realized.[4]

The code was prepared with the view that Indian companies had to adopt the best of corporate practices if they were to access domestic as well as foreign capital at competitive rates. The code agreed that there was no unique way of understanding corporate governance. Different structures established in different countries might not be pertinent to local conditions. With increased exposure to global markets, it became imperative for corporations to focus on transparency and adopt full disclosure mechanisms, apart from consistently directing themselves towards amelioration of shareholder value. However, the code focused specially on the public-listed companies.

Corporate governance practices have gained a great impetus after the adoption of the much-celebrated Securities and Exchange Board of India (SEBI) appointed Kumar Mangalam Birla Committee (KMBC) Report on Corporate Governance. The acceptance and ratification by SEBI, in early 2000, of the KMBC report on corporate governance has paved the way to rationalize and restructure governance practices in corporate India. The SEBI report was a timely intervention to keep a tab on the uninhibited corporate misdemeanors rampant in India. The recommendations were supposed to be enforced through provisions in listing agreements, by local stock exchanges where the companies are listed.[5] However, the report does not bring under its purview unlisted firms, which are mushrooming rapidly. Given the illiquidity of most listed firms, stronger listing norms do not effect any material changes if such firms do not adhere to the mandatory disclosure norms. Only companies that are in the highest bracket and that trade voluminously are affected by such norms and hence try to abide by them.

The new recommendations have forced a dramatic alteration in the disclosure norms for closely-held and/or family-dominated firms. Demands made by the report of certain disclosures and the mandatory setting up of the recommended subcommittees have been the bane of a majority of the listed firms.

The existence of a strong financial press in the country has compelled the law-enforcing bodies to be on their toes. For the past few years, the press has been buttressing the need for disclosure through its financial analysis and revealing stories of corporate misdemeanors.

The pace at which corporate governance practices are being adopted by the industry does cast a doubt on the intentions of both the regulators and the industry. However, adoption of better governance practices cannot be done away with, because the costs attached to non-compliance to global standards would take a heavy toll on those firms that would want to be long-term players.

Historical Evolution of CG: Systemic Development Argument[6]

Pre-Independence Period to the 1970s: Corporate India owes its genesis to the managing agency system that emerged as the bedrock on which Indian economy developed. The genesis of the managing agency system cannot be decisively rooted to some exact date but it is believed that the system evolved as soon as the East India company was dissolved and ceased to trade in 1833.[7]

Managing agency system was a miniature replica of the limited liability company and was so designed that the promotion, finance and administration of companies would be taken care of by the agents in return for a small share of ownership and/or agency fees.[8] After East India Company ceased its operations in India in 1833, it was initially the British merchants who turned into managing agents and with the passage of time indigenous managing agencies sprouted up to act as local agents of the industrial houses and the merchant class of the United Kingdom. British merchants who wanted to set up operations in India appointed managing agents who, in turn, not only provided their masters with capital, managerial labor and share ownership but also technical, social and other physical benefits.[9]

At a time when Indian capital markets were not organized and when the banking system in this country was not well-developed, it befell the managing agencies to play the role of specialized institutions like that of investment bankers of the United States, issue underwriters of the United Kingdom, industrial credit banks of Germany and modern-day venture capitalists.[10] Famous amongst the Indian managing agency houses were Tatas, Birlas, Poddars, Ruias, Narangs, Bhadanis, Sakeserias, Singhanias and Dalmias. Not very surprisingly, these managing agency houses bloomed to become the leading business houses of the country in the time to come.

The managing agencies due to their very nature could bring in technical, financial, personnel and experiential resources to their client companies. Managing agents promoted their client companies after due diligence much similar to the procedure followed by the venture capitalists today. Capital needed to finance industrial development was mobilized by the managing agents despite the absence of an organized capital market in the country. Not only did the managing agents fund the initial investments of their client companies but they also vouched for their clients were they to approach any bank for capital loans. Also, they provided the most important of all resources—management. Though in the initial stages of the evolution of Indian industry, there was an acute shortage of managerial talent and experience, the managing agents could quickly make grounds and cull in qualified personnel to run their clients' businesses. In most cases, the principal agents themselves took care of administration and wore the hats of managers.

Of what is known as the root cause of corporate governance problems in today's context existed even then, in the form of separation of ownership from control. While the managing agents retained control of their client companies, the overseas clients owned the companies. However, it must be mentioned that the managing agents too had a partly minimal stake in ownership, they being providers of the initial investment capital. While tactical or operational decisions were taken by the managing agents, all major policy decisions were supposedly taken by the boards of the managed companies. This concentration of the levels of decision-making was enough to create corporate governance problems. Managing agents with their knowledge of day-to-day activities were in a position to create information asymmetries thus obfuscating the decision-making process of the managed companies.

Astuteness in devising agency contracts helped the managing agents to make provision for centralizing control in their hands. Governance items like that of appointing board of directors, widening operations of the parent firm, making investment decisions, awarding attractive remunerations to themselves lay with the agents. Clauses in the agency contract defining longer terms in office gave the agents unlimited power to veer the direction of the firms as per their volition. This disabled the shareholders to take any conclusive action against the erring agents. More so, clauses like that of the parent firm being penalized for dismissing the agent, gave enough lateral space to the agents to commit corporate governance anomalies.[11]

Underdeveloped capital markets gave the agents leeway to expropriate shareholder wealth. Since the capital was not procured from the capital markets, market discipline could not be imposed upon the agents. Coupled with this was the absence of government regulation to contain the excesses of the agents.

Notorious corporate governance misdemeanors like forcing a profitable company to show losses by transferring the profits as investments into new ventures promoted by the managing agents, and high level of inter-corporate investments resulting in expropriating shareholder value, characterized the way managing agency system functioned during those times.[12] Interlocking directorships helped the firms to indulge in corporate malpractices.[13] Mehta observed that only nine leading industrial families of the country held as many as 600 directorships or partnerships in Indian firms, 100 individuals held 1700 directorships and another 30 persons held as many as 860 directorships indicating the extent to which multiple directorships prevailed in the industry during those times.[14]

Of what has come to be known as the worst abuse of corporate power in modern-day business, the practice of awarding generous perquisites to the directors was rampant during the managing agency system.[15]

Severe corporate governance problems were found to exist under this system and the introduction of The Companies Act of 1956 was basically aimed at containing the exploitation of the shareholders' interests by the managing agents.[16] Malpractices by the managing agents led to a severe crisis in corporate governance and the Act thus came in handy to check and eliminate such problems. Section 146 to section 424 of the Act deal with the management and administration. Sections 324 to 355 contained in Chapter III of the Act deal exclusively with the regulations pertinent to managing agents. The Act abolished the appointment or reappointment of managing agents effective from 3 April 1970.[17] The impact of this legislation suddenly saw the decline in the managing agency system in the country. Table 10.1 depicts how the managing agency system waned from the Indian industry.

Table 10.1 *Diminishing Managing Agency System*

Year	*No. of registered companies*	*No. of companies filed to operate as managing agencies*	*No. of companies permitted to operate as managing agencies*	*Percentage Approval Granted*	*Percentage of managing agencies (as against no. of registered companies)*
1956–57	848	10	10	100	1.2
1957–58	961	11	10	91	1.0
1958–59	1095	01	01	100	0.1
1959–60	1452	06	05	83.3	0.3
1960–61	1683	15	13	86.7	0.8
1961–62	1614	20	19	95	1.2
1962–63	1497	18	13	72.2	0.9
1963–64	1227	11	06	54.5	0.05
1964–65	1366	06	00	00	0
1965–66	1039	01	00	00	0
1966–67	1044	01	00	00	0

Source: Adapted from Sengupta, N.K. (2001), *Government and Business*, pp. 129, Vikas Publishing House Pvt. Limited, New Delhi.

While managing agency system was abolished through the introduction of The Companies Act of 1956, a new system of ownership structure began to evolve in the Indian corporate sector that has come to be known as 'business house'.

The Period from 1970s to 1990s: Though the Companies Act of 1956 abolished the managing agency system effective from the 3 April 1970, yet quite long before its abolition, a new kind of ownership structure emerged in the Indian business scene.[18] While the government retained most strategic industries, the private sector saw the emergence of a new class of owners. Neo-rich managing agents coupled with some capitalist families took over the reins of private sector in the country.[19] The evolution of this class marked the beginning of the emergence of a new form of nexus between politics and business.[20] The new class of owners supported and encouraged the government to adopt an import-substituting industrialization policy to further their own interests of conducting business in a protected environment. Also national leaders and the government of that time were reluctant to allow the market forces to influence the economic outcomes.

Capitalist families have supposedly funded the Congress party in its fight against the imperial rule, and the benefits were later reaped after the party assumed power, post-Independence. Political activities of the Congress party that included social welfare activities were generously supported by the industrialists. In his book, *The Discovery of India*, Nehru conceded that contributions were solicited by the Congress party to contest national and provincial elections in 1937. The fruits of pre-Independence support to the party that would later come into power could be enjoyed by the industry post Independence.[21]

In the post-Independence period, politico-business nexus could be observed in the form of campaign financing by the Indian corporates. The State-business linkage helped the corporations to bargain for special privileges. Industrial Licensing laws that deterred companies from expanding or changing their capacity without prior approval by the government could be easily mauled by the big houses that financed the electoral campaigns.

Bardhan in his book *The Political Economy of Development in India,* said: The richer industrialists, having better 'connections' and better access, have got away with the lion's share in the bureaucratic allocations of the licenses, thus pre-empting capacity creation and sheltering oligopolistic profits. In cases where licensing regulations have been directly aimed at them, the big industrial houses have often freely violated these regulations, created unlicensed capacities (as for example, in 46 units of the Birla group alone) and produced far in excess of the quantity permitted. Over the last decades there has not been a single case of any such company being prosecuted for such violations; on the contrary, repeatedly the Government has *ex post* regularized their unauthorized capacity creation.

As Mukherjee and Reed argue in "Perspectives on the Indian Corporate Economy: Exploring the Paradox of Profits", though in the managing agency system lay the roots of corporate governance, it took its most predominant form in the 'business house' model. In the initial period after Independence, it became contingent upon the government to concentrate on heavy industries and to encourage capital goods industries. Huge capital investments needed for such industries thwarted the entry of smaller players into these sectors. Big business houses having the financial muscle grabbed such opportunities, and bargained with the government for better and rewarding sops under the cover of nation building.

Corporate control now lay firmly ensconced in the hands of the erstwhile managing agents or the controlling families who appointed themselves as managing directors or whole-time directors in their firms. Economic concentration that characterized the managing agency system thus remained stable with the new business house model. The only difference between the managing agency model and the business house model was that while in the former the managing agents managed a group of firms for a dominant partner, in the latter they usurped the firms that they earlier managed, both through legitimate and devious methods and established their control over the group.

Consequent upon the new legislations brought about by the Companies Act of 1956, a functional board with a chairman and managing director replaced the managing agent at the apex of the firm's control under this system. However, it must be remembered that the managing agency system too had boards and the board members were handpicked by the managing agents themselves. Hence, the new form of management with the board at the helm was a mere cosmetic change. The locus of control, however, was not affected. Families still held sway over their firm or the group of firms managed by them.

Interestingly, the business house system was characterized by the existence of a central promoter who invested a bare minimum in the equity capital while garnering monetary resources from various financial intermediaries. While the interventionist approach of the government, on the one hand, fuelled entrepreneurial growth and simultaneously balked economic growth, on the other hand, bureaucratic controls and excessive regulation encouraged underhand dealings, thus strengthening the roots of corporate mis-governance. Controls over production, imports, location, investment and management encouraged industry to resort to a circuitous route to jump legislation. Opportunities for corruption were created, plugging which became a major problem in the reform area.

To develop and bolster industry, the government of the day took the initiative of establishing public financial institutions like the Industrial Credit and Investment Corporation of India (ICICI), Industrial Finance Corporation of India (IFCI) and Industrial Development Bank of India (IDBI). Apart from these, the nationalization of banks and the reforms thereby brought about in the banking sector led to the commercial banks lending industrial credit. On its part, the government also set up investment institutions such as Life Insurance Corporation of India, General Insurance Corporation and the Unit Trust of India that were to bring, at a later stage, a spurt in industrial growth through their investments in industrial equity.[22] The establishment of such financial institutions changed the nature of ownership patterns in the industry. While investment companies directly made it into firms as equity holders, other financial institutions entered into ownership positions by converting their loans into equities.

Nominee directors appointed by the public financial institutions to the boards of companies in which they hold substantial equities have proved that the locus of control in the firm matters in corporate governance. While the nominee directors were expected to voice dissent in case of any misappropriation of public wealth or any mis-governance, it has been seen that they have always remained passive directors or, if active, have supported the management in their actions. Thus, despite fractionated ownership, family management seemed to control the organization. A further change in industry ownership could be observed with the development of capital markets.[23] The public started investing in the industry through the stock markets and a new class of ownership emerged in the form of retail shareholders. These shareholders, however, could not take 'control' of the firm in their hands. Instead, they had to entrust their control to the management (once again the family or the apex group) and be content with the annual dividend. Merchant summarizes corporate control as "unless one belongs to the 'charmed circle' of the family or friends of the existing management, which more often than not, has only a minor share interest in the company, one has no chance whatsoever of becoming a director, however competent one might be."[24] This shows that the new class of owners could not displace the initial promoters from management (and control) positions. Despite their small holdings, the apex group or the family managers managed to control the firms.

Given the government's developmental drives, product competition was ruled out. With no serious competitors around who could give a price fight, business houses reaped enormous profits. Profits thus made were very rarely found to be ploughed back into societal welfare causes. Softer loans from financial institutions meant that business houses did not need to resort to the capital market and hence shareholder disciplining was out of question. While the listed companies came under the purview of disclosures, private companies made the most of the lax legislations as well as inefficient legal system.[25]

Unlike other developing countries where the capitalist structure is marked by the presence of foreign capital, Indian development was wary of foreign presence. Foreign managing agencies that existed before Independence either sold off to their Indian partners or else continued their operations with sullenness. The interventionist approach of the government restricted foreign capital in Indian industry. However, multinational corporations were allowed to hold a maximum of 49% stake in their Indian subsidiaries.[26] This form of protection directly resulted in strengthening the clout of corporate control in the hands of family management or the apex group.

While reforms were rather necessary to bring about some discipline in corporate management, the economic shock of 1990s saw the country liberalizing its economy. Though the established business houses could not be displaced, new forms of management could be observed in companies. Professionals took over the industry by storm and this trend could be observed even in family businesses.[27] Business houses and family businesses that were earlier exclusively managed by the family members and/or the apex group, now changed hands and professionals took control of the management. However, it was only the management that the professionals took over; the control still lay with the business houses or the family. A new class of owners now made their way into the shareholding pattern. Employees of corporations bought shares either through open markets or were awarded stock options by the companies through which they came to own a part of the corporation.

1990s and Thereafter: Corporate governance came under the prism of international pressure with the adoption of reforms in the country. While Part VI of the Companies Act of 1956 extensively covered corporate governance issues, the degree to which they were to be complied with was found missing. Lax government regulations, underhand dealings, business-politics nexus and inefficient judicial system encouraged bad governance practices in the industry. The general economic reforms brought about a change in formalizing the mechanism through announcements of stringent action in case of non-compliance with the provisions of the Act.

Entry of multinational corporations into the country, the huge growth of Indian corporate houses, an upsurge in start-ups and new ventures by enterprising entrepreneurs, the emergence of a new class of financiers, namely, venture capitalists, increase in the number of management training institutions, birth of a new creed of professionally qualified human resource, demands and disciplining effect of capital markets, urgent demand for specialists to arrest product market needs and conducive government regulations helped bring about a change in corporate management. Professional managers took over the day-to-day operations from family managers. With reputation and careers at stake, these managers focused "excessively" on performance and value deliverables. Focus on delivering shifted from annual reports to quarterly performance reports. Capital markets kept a close vigil on non-performing companies and punished them, though not quite often.[28]

To avoid getting entangled in the mire of market-based punishment mechanisms like hostile takeovers, forced acquisitions, poor performance ratings, and with the ready availability of managerial resource, managers became more and more myopic in their dispensation. This myopia led to the adoption of circuitous routes to circumvent being projected as weak performers. Decisions taken by these professionals to increase company wealth thus had serious repercussions on the community at large. While the shareholders are the primary stakeholders of the company, the decisions taken by the company management seemed to affect a whole lot of other stakeholders such as workers, consumers, community, government, suppliers and future generation.[29] This called for an urgent need to recast the governance practices in Indian corporations.

While academics and practitioners believed that the Indian industry had come of age and family-management gave way to professional management, governance purists have announced that Indian industry has begun to model itself on the Anglo-American system of governance.

Though separation of ownership and control could be theoretically observed in Indian industry after the economic reforms (and in some cases even before the reforms process was initiated), in reality, the locus of control still lay with the promoter-owners. Professional managers had to follow the diktats of the family members and the corporation's vision was necessarily that of the owners'. While the creation of information asymmetries by the managers is a phenomenon peculiar to the Anglo-American model of governance, in India, managers have mostly failed to do so. In family-dominated businesses, information asymmetries were created by the managers in connivance with the promoters. The information asymmetries thus created were used to shield their mis-governance from the markets and the retail shareholders.

Family dominance in corporate governance has seemingly negated the birth of free managerial capitalism in this country. Differences between the professional managers and the family or promoter always resulted in the former bearing the brunt of the latter's ire. The sacking of Sunil Alagh, Britannia Industries' charismatic chief executive officer by the promoter of the company and eminent industrialist, Nusli Wadia, in June 2003, is reminiscent of the dominance of the family in the corporate boards of the country.[30]

Thus the concept of managerial revolution in Indian industry is at best illusionary. As mentioned earlier, though professionals took over the corporate management, the control largely lay in the hands of the promoter-owners or the apex groups. While corporate financial performance largely depended on the abilities of the professional managers, corporate direction was the stronghold of the corporate controllers i.e., the promoters and the apex group.[31] Initiatives of social responsibility were largely the domain of the controllers. Wherever the controlling group has shown some interest in increasing the wealth and value of the other stakeholding groups, the corporations have emerged as trendsetters in adopting corporate governance practices. The lead taken by Tata Iron and Steel Company (a Tata Sons company) in the 1980s, apropos of social welfare, has set pace for many like-minded controlling groups to contribute to societal development.[32]

DISCUSSION QUESTIONS

1. What do you mean systemic evolution of corporate governance?
2. Discuss the role played by managing agents in corporate mis-governance in India.
3. "The post-liberalization period in India has seen separation of ownership and control". Discuss.

NOTES

1. Mishra, R.K. and B. Navin, (2000), "Corporate Governance and Public Enterprise Boards, Productivity", Vol. 40, No. 4, January–March, pp. 544–49.
2. Readers may please note that amongst the institutional investors in developing countries like India, banks play a central role in financing the corporate sector.
3. For a more practical discussion, refer to Godbole, M., (2002), "Corporate Governance: Myth and Reality", *Economic and Political Weekly*, 27 July–2 August, 2002, Vol. 37, No. 30, pp. 3094–3102.
4. For details, refer to CII, (1998) Desirable Corporate Governance: A Code.
5. For a detailed report, refer to SEBI, (2000) Draft Report of the Kumar Managalam Committee on Corporate Governance. This report is also available on http://www.sebi.com/report/corpgovern.html.
6. For a related and rigorous study, refer to Mukherjee, A. and D. Reed, (1998), "Three Historical Models and their Development Impact",

in Reed, D. and S. Mukherjee, edited *Corporate Governance, Economic Reforms, and Development: The Indian Experience*, Oxford University Press.

7. Refer to Anstey, Vera, (1929), *The Economic Development of India*, Longmans, Green and Company, London, for an interesting exposition. Rungta (1970) however maintains that managing agency system can be dated back to 1809. The system, however, has supposedly gained currency after the Indian Companies Act of 1850 was passed.
8. In the early days, the managing agents received poundage, which meant that a certain percentage (usually 5%) on the total sales went to them. Later, they started receiving percentage on the total profits, and with the advent of time, the managing agents came to possess a small share of the parent company of which they were the agents. However, it must be remembered that initially managerial control lay with the managing agents.
9. The other kind of benefits included that of laying and providing transportation facilities for the transfer of goods from one place to the other; arranging for and mobilizing capital as and when needed; liaising locally with third parties for their foreign masters; providing ancillary facilities like shipping and insurance. Given the kind of activities that the managing agents were undertaking, it was quite clear that they performed the functions of overseas managers.
10. See also Kuchhal, S.C., (1960), *The Industrial Economy of India*, Chaitanya Publishing House, Allahabad, India, p. 397.
11. For a better understanding of how managing agencies functioned during the colonial period, refer to Mukherjee Reed, A., (2001), *Perspectives on the Indian Corporate Economy: Exploring the Paradox of Profits*, Palgrave: New York.
12. Refer to Government of India, (1963), Report of Justice Vivian Bose Commission, which directs us to the observation that funds were accumulated from those companies of which the D. J. Group was the managing agent for the benefit of the private companies in which the group had interests. The commission report states: "…in these cases it was always the public companies that suffered and the investing public along with them. The wrong lay in the fact that those who were in control wrested improper advantage for themselves from the companies that they controlled and let the companies under their control suffer."
13. Which has been recognized by the modern-day lawmakers as a serious problem and is considered to be one of the primary reasons for anomalies in corporate governance.

14. For a detailed study, see Mehta, M.M. (1952), *The Combination Movement in Indian Industries*, Friends' Book Depot: Allahabad.
15. By 'directors' I mean the managing agents who awarded themselves perquisites in excess of their needs under the pretext of administrative expenses (Sharma and Chauhan, 1965). This problem of excess remuneration has been taken seriously after the reforms. Market discipline coupled with shareholder voice have compelled the government to slap a legislation of disclosure in this regard.
16. By shareholders, in this context, I mean the managed companies or the client companies of the managing agencies.
17. Following the I.G. Patel Managing Agency Inquiry Committee report, the Central government abolished the agency system in five industries viz., sugar, paper, cotton, textiles and jute. Managing agencies in the rest of the industries have been phased out w.e.f. 3 April 1970.
18. By new kind of ownership, I essentially mean that ownership has only undergone a cosmetic change and has become more visible than ever. The managing agents who had earlier managed a group of firms now took control of the firms. They regrouped themselves as an umbrella and adopted the company form of management.
19. The empires of Tata, Wadia, Kirloskar and Godrej started way back in the late nineteenth century or early 1900s. Other prominent business houses viz., Mafatlal, Shriram, Birlas, Hinduja, Singhanias, Bajaj, Thapars, Piramal, Lalbhai, Goenkas, Mahindras and others evolved between 1900 and 1947. These houses gained strength after Indian Independence and took advantage of all the sops made available by the government to bolster the country's economy. Interestingly, most of these empires were leading managing agency houses which accumulated enough wealth to start out on their own as huge industrial houses. Mehta (1952) documents that the Tatas, Birlas, Singhanias, Thapars and Goenkas controlled as many as 26, 24, 42, 32 and 14 companies respectively under the managing agency form.
20. While the existence of such a nexus cannot be denied in a period prior to this, yet it was during this period that the business learnt to exploit government legislations in its favor. While the managing agency system too had such attendant problems of a close nexus with the government, yet the benefits to the agency could not be corroborated by the agents as easily as they could be under the business house model. The pre-Independence nature of government-business nexus was more in favor of the British rule and even legislations were made to support British

interests. However, the astuteness with which the Indian managing agents cornered the loci of control is something worth understanding.

21. In the words of Kobrak (2002), "Cozy political arrangements are serious enough in that they pork up legislation, provide contributors with overly generous returns on their investments, courtesy of their taxpayers, initiate superfluous programs and perpetuate outmoded activities." For an interesting read on campaign finance and political governance please see Kobrak, P. (2002), *Cozy Politics: Political Parties, Campaign Finance, and Compromised Governance*, Lynne Reinner Publishers, London.
22. However, the UTI scam of 2001 was one of the most blatant forms of corporate misgovernance which drew the attention of the investing public that even government institutions are not to be trusted with public savings.
23. The repeal of Capital Issues Control Act (1947) in 1992 contributed to the stock market boom and public shareholding grew in leaps and bounds.
24. Merchant, K. T. (1970), "Management Change in Companies", *Economic and Political Weekly*, 5, 23, pp. 921–23.
25. However it does not necessarily mean that public companies abided by the code. Serious lapses were found in their reporting and disclosures. Yet listed companies stood the chance of serious scrutiny in case of any anomaly.
26. The liberalization reforms saw a change in the policy apropos of foreign capital. With increasing investments by foreign institutional investors post-1991 and their subsequent dissonance in investing more due to bad corporate governance practices prevalent in Indian industry, further reforms in corporate management had to be brought in.
27. For an interesting study on family business and their business practices, see Dutta, S. (1997), "Family Business in India", *Response Books*, New Delhi.
28. The trend of stock markets disciplining corporate management for non-performance has slowly begun. However, there are many companies that get away with their bad performance riding on the crest of 'free rider system.' Shareholders have of late started behaving like investors who provide companies with risk capital. In case of their dissonance with companies in which they have invested, they have two options: voice or exit. Shareholders prefer to exit from the holding equity positions in the company for voice has its own attendant disadvantages viz., lack of shareholder unity and free rider benefits (while one

shareholder may move the courts for justice, the others stand to benefit without putting in any efforts).

29. The stakeholder theory gained currency with business press, non-governmental organizations and others voicing their dissent vehemently and more loudly. Otherwise, the earlier models were not devoid of stakeholder value expropriating practices. While every ownership model tried to maximize its profits, yet with the growing influx of international best practices, managerial capitalism was victimized for not conforming to better corporate governance norms.
30. Similar other examples of family dominance and control of Indian corporations and their intolerance towards professional management can be recounted in the Indian governance context. The most notable amongst them being that of the tussle between erstwhile TISCO chairman Rusi Mody and the scion of Tata Sons, Ratan Tata. For a story on the Alagh episode, see "The Cookie crumbles for Sunil Alagh at Britannia," *The Economic Times*, 5 June 2003.
31. Corporate ownership and corporate control are two very important concepts that have been debated by academic researchers for quite some-time. While ownership is quantifiable, control is not. Hence, while discussing issues of corporate governance, it makes sense to identify the locus of control. Corporate strategies are chalked out based on the ideologies and motivations of the controlling group. It is possible for an ownership group to hold a nominal equity position in the firm and yet retain corporate control with itself. This is primarily because the other ownership groups are not in a position to organize themselves to take control of the organization or otherwise, do not either have the expertise or interest to possess control. Hence it is observed that the Indian corporate sector is mostly controlled by the promoter-owner or the family despite their measly shareholdings.
32. Some family-dominated business houses like that of Mafatlals, Goenkas, Birlas, Reliance group and even professionally managed companies like Hindustan Unilever Limited (through its programme of integrated rural development), have either contributed liberally to corporate philanthropy or have undertaken many a meaningful project as a part of their corporate social responsibility initiatives.

Chapter 11

Relationship-based Evolution

The previous chapter has explained the organic growth of corporate governance. This chapter looks at the current day corporate governance efforts and then, through some corporate mis-governance instances, traces back the reasons that have pushed the country to adopting better governance practices. It is a new intervention to the existing understanding of the evolution of corporate governance. It starts with Form 49A that is considered to be the only available pro-active mechanism to haul listed companies and subsequently, establishes that government negligence in enforcement coupled with its largesse to the industry is what has created the space for mis-governance.

EXPLAINING THE CONTEXT

Form 49 A of SEBI's listing agreement became a mandatory instrument, post SEBI–KMBC report on corporate governance, to elicit corporate disclosures on a wide range of issues like the composition of the board, financial auditing practices, constitution and composition of various mandated committees, names of the independent directors, amongst others.[1] Despite the implementation of this clause with full pomp and zeal, its enforcement is still a weak link that buttresses the fact that corporations can easily get away without adhering even to the mandated regulations. The recent Satyam fraud is a case in example. The promoter of Satyam has systematically bled the company of its funds by divesting profits, manipulating accounts and arm-twisting the boards.

Compliance in India is an awkward term, a cliché, often referred to by academicians and perhaps of academic interest in the industry. At the height of corporate governance scams, when the government was supposed to be rather stringent in enforcing compliance with its regulations, even bare minimum requirements like filing of annual returns, have shamefully come down year after year.

If the figures depicted in Table 11.1 are any indication, one can understand the sorry state of our enforcement. Table 11.2 depicts how no improvement could be seen in the effective compliance rate.[2]

Table 11.1 *Compliance Rate in Filing Documents*

Year	*Companies*	*Annual Returns Filed*	*Compliance Rate (%)*	*Balance Sheet/P&L Account Filed*	*Compliance Rate (%)*
1994–95	353292	219705	62.19	221832	62.79
1995–96	409142	220318	53.85	201275	49.19
1996–97	450950	247423	54.87	267335	59.28
1997–98	484500	274814	56.72	277000	57.17
1998–99	511990	260530	50.89	270961	52.92

Source: Naresh Chandra Committee Report on Corporate Governance, Department of Company Affairs, Ministry of Justice and Company Affairs, New Delhi, 2002.

Table 11.2 *Net Compliance Rate*

Year	*Compliance in Filing (Annual Returns) in percentage*	*Percentage of documents taken on record*	*Effective Compliance Rate*
1994–95	62.19	50.04	31.12
1995–96	53.85	46.47	25.02
1996–97	54.87	47.22	25.91
1997–98	56.72	54.57	30.95
1998–99	50.89	58.79	29.92

Source: Naresh Chandra Committee Report on Corporate Governance, Department of Company Affairs, Ministry of Justice and Company Affairs, New Delhi, 2002.

Weak enforcements have always been an issue to reflect upon. Successive governments have been very lax in enforcing regulations. If the two tables above are any indication, it suggests the general apathy the government exhibits in taking "non-compliance" to task. One argument could be that the nature of politics is such that nothing can be enforced strictly without jeopardizing politically motivated relationships. There are innumerable opportunity costs involved in strict enforcement of such regulations such as the cost of retaining the support of industrial houses; cost of the future growth; cost of the future political equations; and such other opportunity costs which compel the incumbent government to go lax on some enforcements that could be detrimental to friendly political constituencies.

This chapter examines whether the same kind of laxity existed during the first three and a half decades in the post-Independence period when successive governments were single-party dominated. By probing corporate governance issues, this chapter seeks to unravel the government-industry ties that were a hindrance to the proper and efficient functioning of both the entities.

This chapter picks on six examples to show that corporate mis-governance is a creation of government indifference and its belated response to mis-governance.

While there are a number of legislations pertinent to industry and governance such as MRTP, FERA, licensing policies and industry-specific legislations that one can study to find instances of the government's rather conscious or unconscious abetment of corporate mis-governance, banking business has been singled out to substantiate the argument.[3] Banking stands out as a better explananda of the "abetment" argument due to a variety of reasons. First, banking was a government-run industry. Second, while credit rationing policies were in place, banks have been liberal in dispensing credit to industrialists at the behest of either the State or its machinery. Third, SICA-BIFR enactment provided a fillip to the "debt siphoning" industry. Fourth, it took the government about two decades post-

Independence to nationalize banking industry despite the weaknesses of the then banking system in contributing to the development goals envisaged by the government and then again it took another two decades to initiate reforms in the industry, by which time, private sector could successfully capture and bleed the financial institutions of their coffers. Fifth, while other legislations dealt with the government's control on industry, banking and its associated legislations have contributed to the industry's penchant to practice corporate mis-governance on a large scale till the bubble burst in 1992.

Issues like insider trading, excessive executive compensation, expropriation of shareholders' wealth, false reporting, non-disclosure of certain accounting and governance practices, self-dealing, inter-corporate investments, a high degree of cross-holdings, circuitous routing of loans to non-productive activities, siphoning off public funds and adopting debt defaults as a strategic tool have all emanated due to government's negligence in nipping these kind of problems in the bud. The chapter through its arguments examines the role government played in fostering corporate mis-governance prior to the pre-liberalization period. It explains industry-State nexus and how the banking system of the country contribute as well as get affected by this nexus.

LIC–Mundhra Scam: In what is known as the first scam in free India, Life Insurance Corporation of India (LIC), a government owned entity bought over Rs.12.4 million worth of shares of six companies belonging to Calcutta-based industrialist Haridas Mundhra, under pressure from the government in 1957.[4] While a majority of these shares were fictitious, even the prices at which LIC purchased these shares were more than what Mundhra had asked for.

LIC had bypassed its investment committee to make these purchases, purely under the pressure of the then finance secretary. The investment committee was apprised of this deal only after it was struck, allowing for the committee to conclude that such a huge deal would not be possible for the corporation without the consent of the government.

While the finance minister had maintained his innocence on this issue, Feroze Gandhi, MP and son-in-law of the then prime minister Jawaharlal Nehru, claimed to have had damaging evidence on the confidential correspondence between the minister and his secretary on this issue. Under such public outcry, the prime minister appointed a one-man committee headed by Justice Chagla, who conducted a 24-day public inquiry and held the finance minister, T.T. Krishnamachari, constitutionally responsible for LIC's surreptitious deal. The minister was subsequently forced to resign.

While the finance minister made pleas of ignorance on the nexus between his finance secretary and Mundhra, the government and the LIC claimed that the insurance giant had to jump in to "remove the drag on the market".[5] Financial wizards like A.D. Shroff and Bhagwandas Govardhandas, however, refuted the drag theory. Their contention was that the retail investor was not interested in Mundhra's shares and the Calcutta Stock Exchange was not showing any promise of stock trading. Shroff contended that two types of entities held Mundhra's ten million worth of shares—a horde of banks with whom his shares were pledged and a few brokers. The theory of "market drag" was therefore a sham. The government showed interest in toning up markets that never existed in the first place. More interestingly, the government authorized itself to instruct LIC to digress from its primary responsibility of servicing its policy holders. Two questions that have been asked by generations of corporate theorists are: (i) How could LIC funds be pumped into buying inconsequential shares? and (ii) did LIC hold any market obligations to conduct itself in such a manner?

Surprisingly, LIC had purchased Mundhra's shares despite Bombay Stock Exchange's warning to the investors in 1956 that some of Mundhra's shares were forged and fictitious.

In what might seem very blatant today, the government had informed Mundhra a full three days in advance that his shares would be bought at the closing price of 24 June 1956, giving him room for manipulating and jacking up his share prices on the last day. Such soft corner for an industrialist and the loot of public money to protect him is evidence enough to suggest that the government did its bit either conveniently ignoring good governance practices or had played a deliberate role in abetting corporate mis-governance. Thus were sown the seeds of corporate mis-governance in the country.[6]

Banking proxies and Mis-governance: For over three and a half decades, the banking sector's performance had created a credibility gap in terms of the government's ability to harness the industry controlled by it. The roots of corporate misappropriations lay in the weakness of the banking system as well as in the organized nexus between the trio of banker-businessman-political representative. If post-liberalisation declarations of NPAs are any indication, the banking system in this country has perhaps always been in a deep mess, yet unknown to the public at large, till the bubble burst as an effect of Narsimhan Committee's Report in 1992. While it may be easy to correlate the large-scale defaults of industrialists post-banking-sector reforms to the widespread abetment of corporate mis-governance by the government, the lack of availability of pre-liberalisation literature or data on banking anomalies, throws the study of collecting evidence on government's deliberately played ignoramus' role or willing abetment of a collective loot by the industrialist-banker duo of the public exchequer, out of gear.

Post-Independence banking till the period of nationalization was abundant with corporate governance problems. Lack of conclusive evidence on how business houses have squeezed the banks of loans and to what tune, call for employing of proxies to explain the large-scale expropriation of wealth that has definitely taken place. Thus two major proxies have been employed to explain the phenomenon: directors of banks associated with or having connections with other companies; and percentage credit advanced to farm sector and SSI sector as against the total percentage of bank credit.

These two proxies advance the argument that the government in the early period after Independence has failed in visualizing the magnitude of governance crimes that would subsequently occur due to its negligence in regulating, or else has conveniently managed to ignore these proxies as not important enough to attract immediate regulation.

Modern corporate governance theory extols the virtues of "independent directors" and the need to constitute modern day boards with about half their number. Reasons for this are manifold, the primary reason being to avoid conflict of interests.

Table 11.3 shows a representation of directors on the boards of 6 banks. The figures in the table suggest that amongst the thirty-four directors of these six banks, they had connections with 500 companies.

Table 11.3 *Number of Companies Each Director is Associated With*

No.	*Name of the Director*	*Connection with No. of Companies*
	Bank of India	
1	A.D. Shroff	23
2	K.M.D. Thackersey	28
3	Jugmohan P. Goenka (Goenka Group)	11
4	Jaisingh Vithaldas (Vissanji Khimji Group)	16
5	Girdharilal Mehta (Henderson Mehta Group)	11
6	Ambalal Sarabhai (Sarabhai Group)	16
7	Madan Mohan Mangaldas (Sarabhai Group)	17
8	Bhagwandas C. Mehta (C.V. Mehta Group)	10
9	N.K. Petigara (Solicitor)	12
10	Ramniwas Ruia (Ruia Group)	38
	Central Bank of India	
1	C.H. Bhabha	9
2	C.P. Wadia (Wadia Group)	6
3	S.S. Khambatta (Solicitor)	6
4	Jamshetji Jeejibhoy-Barnet (Industrialist)	9
5	C.B. Parekh (Cotton Merchant)	16
6	Dharamsey Khatau (Khatau Group)	29
7	J. Harivallabhdas (Mill Agent)	21
8	Sir J. M. Scindia (Former Ruler of Gwalior)	8

(Contd)

	Union Bank of India	
1	K.R.P. Shroff	4
2	Balkrishna Harivallabhdas	7
3	Jai H. Mehta (Tata Group)	24
4	Ratilal H. Shah	22
5	Pallanji S. Mistry (Merchant & Contractor)	24
	Punjab National Bank	
1	Kamalnayan Bajaj	21
2	C.L. Bajoria (Dalmia Group)	11
3	A.K. Jain	8
4	S.K. Jain	13
	Bank of Baroda	
1	Naval H. Tata	10
2	Tulsidas Kilachand (Kilachand Group)	11
3	R.B. Birla (Birla)	9
4	K.P. Goenka	15
5	Arvind Mafatlal	15
	United Commercial Bank	
1	E.P. Goenka	12
2	Yogendra M. Mafatlal	8

Source: Blitz—Oct 5, 1964, p. 17.

The Companies Act of 1956 clearly stipulated that no one individual can hold more than 20 directorships across all companies that he has connections with. However, there is not enough evidence to prove whether any specific director listed above did have connections with more than 20 companies or were merely connected to them due to some familial or associative ties. Nevertheless one cannot but openly doubt the organizational accountability of such individuals who had multiple connections and were also on the boards of banks.

Such connections led to a variety of corporate governance problems such as self-dealing; easy loans for companies of disrepute; soft loans for companies close to the directors' heart; pre-approved loans for newer projects without any due diligence; laxity on credit monitoring; laxity on recovery; willful default of loans by companies; and continued protection to the defaulters and further credit extensions to them by the directors.

Reform of the Banking Sector

As early as in 1956, there was hue and cry in the Lok Sabha on the sorry state of affairs in the banking sector. Shri Gurpada Swamy moved a resolution in the lower house of parliament for the nationalization of banks, but the ruling Congress party thwarted it by maintaining that the government held approximately about twenty-two percent of the Indian banking sector through the State Bank of India and had no intentions to further augment its holding. Subsequently a couple of more resolutions were moved in the lower house for nationalization citing reasons like big business expropriation ofbank wealth. However, as usual, two successive finance ministers, Pranab Mukherjee and T.T. Krishnamachari, summarily brushed aside the issue with their curt remarks.[7]

In 1960, the bankruptcy of Laxmi Bank Limited and Palai Central Bank Limited had scarred the government; even then lessons were not learnt. Instead, amendments were made to the Banking Companies Act and the RBI Act in 1961 and 1962, plugging the loopholes in the banking legislation and giving more powers to the Reserve Bank of India.

A look at Tables 11.4 and 11.5 throw light on the preferential credit allocations that big business received during the early decades of post-Independence. While the agriculture sector never crossed four percent credit allocation for the period shown below, the small scale industries sector averaged at about 5.4% if 1967 figures are not reckoned. The total credit to these two sectors averaged between eight percent and twelve percent of the total bank credit. A major question that now arises is: who was the beneficiary of the other 90%?

Table 11.4 *Share of Farm Sector in Bank Credit*

Period	*% farm credit against total bank credit*
March 1956	2%
April 1961	3.1%
March 1966	2.4%
March 1967	2.1%

Source: Verma, J.C. (1971), *Nationalization of Banks in India: a Detailed Analysis of Schemes and Proposals*, Career Digest Publications, New Delhi.

Table 11.5 *Share of Credit to SSIs as Percentage of Total Bank Credit*

Period	*% farm credit against total bank credit*
December 1960	5.1%
December 1961	5.0%
December 1962	4.4%
March 1965	5.9%
March 1966	6.2%
March 1967	10.2%

Source: Verma, J.C. (1971), *Nationalization of Banks in India: a Detailed Analysis of Schemes and Proposals*, Career Digest Publications, New Delhi.

By the then Union Minister of Planning, Ashok Mehta's admission in 1966, about 650 borrowers constituted nearly two-thirds of the beneficiaries of the total advances made by the banking system.[8] While the government was aware of such a huge debacle where nearly two-thirds of bank credit was parked with just about 650 borrowers in a country of over 400 million people, why was it not willing to rein in the banking sector? If minister Mehta's statement in 1966 is read in conjunction with Table 11.3, it becomes evident that the government did not consider it serious enough to look into the governance issues that could emerge out of the bank directors' multiple connections with other companies. Some questions that arise are: Why was it willingly deflecting from taking any action, or for that matter passing any legislation? Why had the government to wait till 1969 to nationalize some banks? Surprisingly, the political party that had vehemently opposed nationalization on the pretext of imprudence in running the banks, took a full U-turn to nationalize them just six years later after T.T.K.'s adverse remarks on nationalization. T.T.K, the then Finance Minister in response to the resolution moved in 1963 for nationalization had remarked, "...there is no need for nationalizing the banking industry since the direct or immediate gain to the government in the form of additional income, after the payment of compensation could not be very great".[9]

It becomes clear from the banking proxies argument that continued conscious negligence by the government has been the root cause for later day large-scale misappropriations. While though not outwardly explicit, the government may be held responsible for sowing the seeds of mis-governance and for scaling up the momentum in a nationwide loot of finances by a handful of big industrialists.

Nationalization of Banks and Stepping up Mis-governance: The movement that spurred the demand for nationalization of banks culminated in 1969 when the then Prime Minister Indira Gandhi's government took the reins of fourteen banks with the idea of breaking the backbone of the banker-businessman nexus. The government had until then conveniently ignored the malady of banks when money was being siphoned off by those who controlled the banks, when insider lending was a norm rather than an exception and when bankruptcy glaringly stared private banks in the face. What is more, the government turned a blind eye even after it was forced to bail out more than ten banks from huge defaults by amalgamating them with the State-held State Bank of India.[10] Finally when realization dawned that the development vision of the government was not being met, apropos of growth of priority sector, it took a serious U-turn and considered nationalization as the only alternative to give an upward thrust to the economy.

With the first round of nationalization in 1969, public sector banks controlled as much as 86% of the country's banking business. This figure further got bolstered by six percentage points to 92% after the second round of nationalization in 1980. So it was effectively the government that was grossly involved in credit allocations through its banks in the post-nationalization period.

The raison d' etre for nationalization was fourfold: the existing banking set-up did not percolate to the interiors of the country and hence there was a need to expand banking system through the length and breadth of the country in order to tap people's savings; massive infrastructure investments required by big business could be funded if a systematic tapping of such savings was done; priority sector lending could be encouraged thereby leading to a growth in small sector and agricultural sector; green revolution that resulted in the aftermath of

1967 famine needed financial dosages for commercial inputs for agriculture.[11] The latter two objectives were considered to be far more important than the first two. How far have these objectives been met has become a matter of immense concern, if some figures were to be recalled for justifying this act of nationalization.

Arvind mentions a few figures in his illuminative paper titled "Banking in India takes a Full Circle" through which one can conclude that the actual objectives with which banks were nationalized were not met. Of the total credit allocation, the share of priority sector has not changed drastically despite the lending provisions set up by the government. If our figures for the year 1967 in Tables 11.4 and 11.5 were our departing point to calculate the credit allocated to priority sector (which is 12.3% of the total credit allocation), the year 1969 was just about the same at 12.2% and alarmingly, three decades after nationalization i.e., in 1999, it was just about 14.4%. This goes on to show how nationalization has helped big business in expropriating a new set of money-lenders—the common people who saved their hard-earned money in public sector banks.

One of the primary reasons for such a lapse is the government's continued abetment of corporate mis-governance. During nationalization, the government's deliberate choice of not tinkering around with the banks' management and allowing it to retain its old set-up did more harm than good.[12] While the board was reconstituted with some directors drawn from the 'public', it was always either the industrialists or businessmen or politicians who qualified themselves as being from the public. Thus the incidence of independence in the board was almost always nil.

Credit started to be directed through large-scale political intervention and what started as loaning to individuals took the shape of mass loans granted to groups of people at the behest of politicians under the pretext of loan melas.[13] Of the corporate sector, Sucheta Dalal says, "a combination of political patronage and widespread corruption allowed the corporate sector to get away with willful default even as it continued to borrow through other companies. All signs of potential sickness and weak feasibility were simply ignored."

Financing Private Sector: The government never had the premonition that what it considered to be a wise step during Independence would under more extenuating circumstances turn into a big blunder. With a view to pocket public savings, the government had introduced controls on private sectors' issuance of corporate shares to the public at large through the Controller of Capital Issues. Not only the quantum, but also the prices at which these shares were issued, were controlled by the government. Since prices of these shares were based on the past profits of the companies and not on the future potential, promising companies had no choice but to access capital from other sources. It is here that the development financial institutions such as Industrial Finance Corporation of India, Industrial Development Bank of India and Industrial Credit and Investment Corporation of India got to play a major role.

From the time of inception, these DFIs were driven by the principle of fostering industrialization in the country. Goswami states that this could be achieved only by advancing long-term loans, mostly at subsidized rates for setting up plant and machinery. The parameter to judge these financial institutions was not their asset quality but, surprisingly, the amount of previous loans sanctioned and disbursed. With such a lax performance recognition measure in place, and with tight government controls over industry in terms of licensing, import-substitution and other kinds of restriction, the industrial financing industry was ensnared with crony capitalism and DFIs were doling out funds to businesses without any proper credibility checks.

Both Patibandla and Goswami in two separate research papers concur that collusion between banker-industrialist-political representatives is a fallout of the dirigistic policies of the State. Financial institutions were captured by the industrialists, loans taken for some particular venture were diverted to some other ventures and later bankruptcy filed. It was the inherent weakness in bankruptcy implementation laws that led to the accumulation of huge non-performing assets by these institutions at a later date. Weaknesses in implementation have also given enough space to the business houses to indulge in corporate mis-governance.

Who then was the majority stakeholder in the private sector? A peek into Table 11.6 throws light on the changing ownership structure in the Indian private corporate sector.

Table 11.6 *Ownership Pattern in India's Private Corporate Sector*

Category of owners	*1959*	*1965*	*1978*	*1982*	*1989*	*1993*	*1996*	*1999*
Nominee Companies, Promoters, Directors	39.6	13	13.8	24	26	30	35	41.79
Financial Institutions and others	7.1	20.3	27.4	30	36.5	32	21	14.25
Trustee and Charitable Institutions	1.2	1.3	1.2	2	1.5	n.a.	n.a.	n.a.
Overseas (Individuals and Institutions)	n.a.	21.3	20.3	n.a.	n.a.	12	13	10.67
Individuals and Public	52.1	44.1	37.3	44	36	26	31	33.31
Total	100	100	100	100	100	100	100	100

Source: Adapted from Panchali, J. and Desai, N. (1999), "Ownership Structure and Financial Performance", in Ravi Kumar, T. edited "Research Papers in Applied Finance" *The ICFAI Journal of Applied Finance*, Hyderabad.

Interestingly, the data in the table provides some insights into how the government has had a major exposure to the private sector for about three decades. And these were the decades when the DFIs and commercial banks had played a major role in fostering industrialization. Funds that were generated by the government through public savings and public taxes found their way into corporations by way of loans from the government financial institutions. In addition, individuals and the public who had money in excess of their bank savings pumped it into the private sector. So, effectively, it was the public either by direct means or through their representative, the government, that was holding a majority stake in the private corporate sector.

If the period between 1965 and 1993 is reckoned, the total exposure of public savings was averaging at about 34% of the total capital exposure as against the promoters' capital exposure of just about 21%. If later day NPAs of Rs.150,000 crores are any indication, then the government's failure in containing such a large-scale expropriation of public money by the industrialists is conspicuous. Growth in the government's exposure to the private sector can be gauged through the continued increase in equity holding by the financial institutions held by the government for the timelines mentioned above till 1993. Between 1959 and 1989, the growth of government-held financial institutions' presence in the corporate private sector increased by about 30 percentage points.

A study by Goswami of 397 listed companies, ranked according to their market capitalisation, shows that even nine years after liberalization, government's exposure to equity still averages at about 20.1%.[14]

Under the guise of fostering industrial development, DFIs were lending funds to big industrialists at the behest of political representatives. As the DFIs were allowed to book their interest income on accrual basis rather than on actual realization, books of accounts never looked like they were cooked up, since income recognition and asset classification were never an issue until the NPA bubble burst. Moreover, nothing was lost for the DFIs for they could extend an even bigger loan amount to the bankrupt industrialist that could help him pay back his earlier dues to the bank, if at all he did and also once again attempt at reorganizing his business.

In Hilton Root's words,

> politicians may ask financial institutions to support existing management in the event of a takeover threat or when the firm lacks adequate collateral, which is a frequent occurrence. Because murky deals are best for generating unaccountable funds, an absence of adequate accounting occurs. Inadequate accounting makes it

difficult for firms to verify their assets; hence corporations often find they require political backers to help get the credit they need from the State-run banking system.

Later day problems of the financial institutions were primarily because the government never considered credit monitoring as important as credit lending. As Khanna and Palepu contend that the financial institutions were under the instructions of the government to take side with corporate management should any dispute arise. Hence, despite having their nominee director on the board of companies, financial institutions never bothered to pull up company management in case of any misappropriation. Instead, as Khanna and Palepu remark, "pouring more money after a bad loan, in the hope that the distressed firm would find its way out of trouble, was consistent with the objective of maximizing loans. Further, this was often a preferable course of action given the difficulty of shutting down failing firms under the Sick Industrial Companies Act". This goes on to show how the government played a major role in shaping up corporate mis-governance in the country and how the industry conveniently played along.

The role of the government in the abetment of corporate crime can also be deciphered from the government-appointed nominees on the boards of the term-lending institutions. Industrialists who were "drawn from the public" by the government to be on the boards of financial institutions were many a time corporate criminals who had fleeced the institutions that they were involved with and yet continued to enjoy the support of the government.

Kulwant Rai of the Usha Group was on the board of the Industrial Development Bank of India and it was during his term with this institution that large amounts of money were siphoned off into some mindless ventures by his group.[15] While his Malvika steel was seeing red and IDBI had no chance of recovering its dues, not a single chairman had the audacity to question Rai on the dues to be paid up.

This certainly supports the argument that the State-industry nexus has been so strong that corporate mis-governance was more of the State's creation, even before all the hue and cry on corporate governance began in the post-liberalization period.

An Alibi Called BIFR: As we progressed through the decades, corporate mis-governance became even more entwined with the State's actions in connivance with the industry. Otherwise, there is no justification for the huge numbers of public and private sector companies being referred to the Board of Industrial and Financial Reconstruction under the provisions of Sick Industrial Companies Act of 1985. As Naik points out, "the Sick Industrial Companies Act and the Board for Industrial and Financial Reconstruction have played a notorious role in providing an easy shelter to defaulters rather than in reviving the sick units". Loans have turned bad not so much because of unforeseen changes in the business environment but because of the easily available opportunity to default. Omkar Goswami Committee Report on Industrial sickness and Corporate Restructuring, in its preamble has aptly mentioned: "There are sick companies, sick banks and unpaid workers. But there are hardly any sick promoters. There lies the heart of the matter".[16]

Based on the recommendations of a Committee of Experts under the chairmanship of T. Tiwari, SICA was enacted as a special legislation by the Government of India in 1985 with the objective of determining sickness and expediting the revival of potentially viable units or closure of units. While the rationale for this has been that revival would translate to productive use of idle investments and closure would mean redirecting the locked-up investment into some other productive purposes, figures on the speed with which cases were dealt with, by any admission, is outrageous. With just about eight percent revival rate of the referred sick companies, SICA has proved that it contained within it the germs of corporate governance cataclysm.

As BIFR asserts,

> securing timely detection of sick and potentially sick companies, the speedy determination by a body of experts of the preventive, ameliorative, remedial and other measure [sic] which need to be taken with respect to such companies and the expeditious enforcement of the measures so determined and for matters connected therewith or incidental thereto.

This process under SICA which is directed and supervised by the Board for Industrial and Financial Reconstruction, shows how appalling the system of detection and correction could be in a community mired with deliberate default designs. By its own admission, BIFR takes about five to seven long years to revive sick companies, and as mentioned earlier, with just about eight percent revival rate and over Rs.1032 billion accumulated losses in the over two decades of its existence, endorsement of SICA–BIFR process by the government is reason enough for one to believe the government's deliberate abetment of corporate mis-governance in the country. Coupled with the losses as reflected in the BIFR process, if NPAs of over Rs.1500 billion were to be reckoned, then it is possible to argue that a major chunk of the country's banking NPAs resulted from the gargantuan delays that the BIFR mechanism took to close a referred case.

Section 22 of the Sick Industrial Companies (Special Provisions) Act, 1985, provides that once a sick company is referred to the BIFR, no proceedings for (a) winding up such a company; (b) for execution of the properties of such company, or (c) the appointment of receiver thereof, and (d) no suit filed for recovery of money, can be effected, except with the consent of BIFR.[17] As Vittal mentions, in the initial years of SICA's implementation, many industries were apprehensive that creditors would lay claim to the property, hence being referred to BIFR was considered to be a scary affair. But once realization dawned that BIFR could be turned into a convenient alibi with Section 22 of SICA as their trump card, more and more companies helped themselves by getting referred to the BIFR. Debt default became a potent instrument to declare bankruptcy with BIFR providing an easy escape route.

Figures 11.1 and 11.2 indicate the number of companies that were referred to the BIFR from 1987 to 2003/4. Though initially

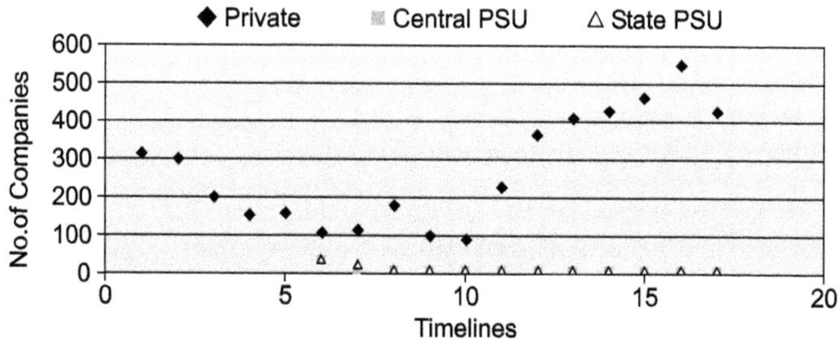

Figure 11.1 *BIFR-referred Cases from 1987 to 2003 (Private Sector, Central PSUs and State PSUs)*

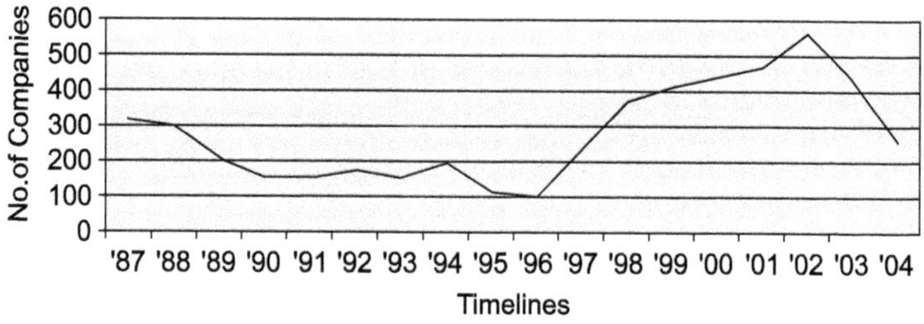

Figure 11.2 *BIFR Cases from 1987 to 2004*

the numbers were on the higher side due to a quick identification of sick industries, gradually the numbers came down due to apprehensions in the industry about likely capture of the assets by creditors. But once it was established that the mean delay time for arriving at any decision by the BIFR was as long as 851 days (for the period 1987–1992)[18] and that Section 22 could be turned to its advantage, promoters adopted debt default as a strategy and led their companies towards bankruptcy, so as to be referred to BIFR.[19] This was the time when NPAs in the banking industry started surfacing as a result of disclosures made by banks on the total exposure they had to bad loans and willful defaulters. Figures 11.3, 11.4 and 11.5 suggest that the private sector has managed the glory of being referred to the BIFR much more than the public sector. Also the net worth of the private sector that came under the purview of BIFR stands at Rs.43230.72 crores as against Central Public Sector Units' Rs.9055.93 crores and State Public Sector Units' Rs.2364.25 crores. While these figures may squarely thrust blame on the private sectors' expropriation of public money, the public sector, however, cannot be spared of reproach if the net accumulated losses to the net worth ratio were to be taken into consideration. As against the private sectors' accumulated losses of Rs.78131.95 crores over its net worth, shamefully the Central and State Public Sector Units have done more damage to the economy.[20]

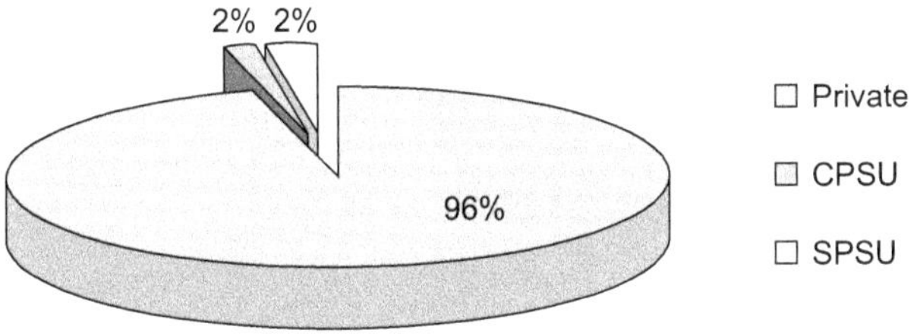

Figure 11.3 *Cases Referred to BIFR*

Following Figure 11.6, the government has to be first blamed for squandering public money on such a massive scale. Together, the

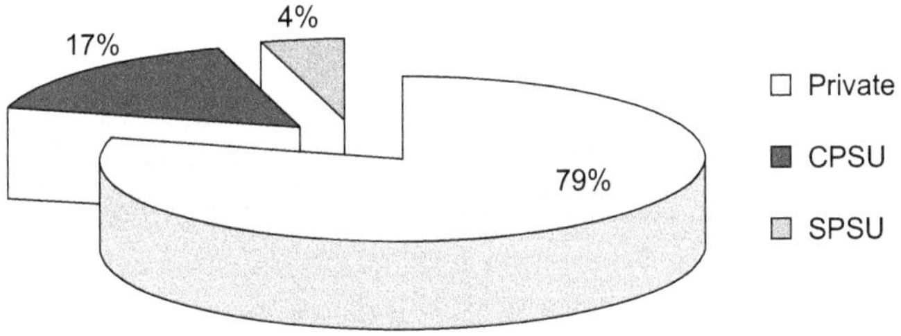

Figure 11.4 *Net Worth Ownership-wise*

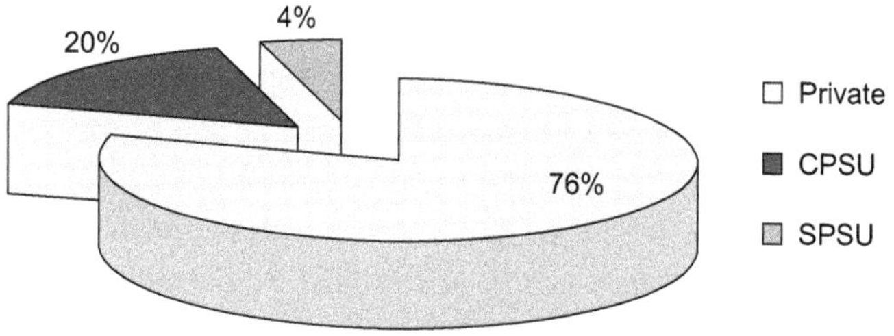

Figure 11.5 *Accumulatd Losses of the Referred Cases (Ownership-wise)*

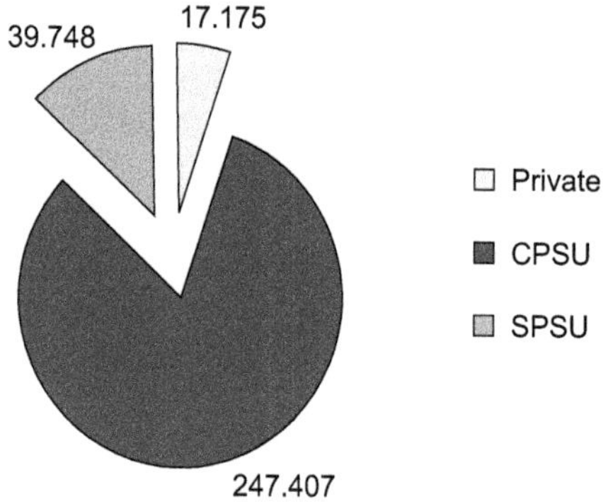

Figure 11.6 *Per Unit Accumulated Loss (Ownership-wise) for all BIFR Cases Referred*

public sector units have registered over Rs.287 crores of accumulated loss per unit that has been referred to the BIFR (Central PSUs at a per unit accumulated loss of Rs.247.40 crores and State PSUs at Rs.39.75 crores), against the private sectors' per unit accumulated loss of Rs.17.18 crores. These comparative figures could have spoken still more disastrously for the government-run organisations, had the PSUs been referred to BIFR right from 1987 which is when the private sector was being referred to.[21] While the hue and cry on the NPAs being a creation by the private sector may hold good for public debate, the large scale loot of public exchequer by the government-run public sector units indicate the government's role in building up corporate mis-governance in the country.

To quote DFID: "Where there are no rules the rich and powerful bully the poor and the powerless". Indian corporate governance has always been besmirched by the rich (businessmen) and powerful (State and its machinery).[22] While the State was relentlessly emptying its own coffers by running its companies with a high degree of inefficiency, the industry never stopped in milking the cash cows that went by the name of financial institutions and commercial banks. Unsurprisingly, the loot affected the public at large, while as mentioned earlier "...there are hardly any sick promoters".

Non-Performing Assets and CG: While BIFR–SICA process provided an alibi for the industrialists to bleed the banks, the banks too were mired in systemic failures in their lending practices. Under the cover of the provisions made in Banking Secrecies Act, banks have been able to withhold the names of debt defaulters. This section probes the factors that contributed to the growing non-performing assets in the banking industry.

With over Rs.1500 billion as non-performing assets in the nation's banking industry, the government's governance delinquencies were never more outrageous. Squandering public money in the name of development, encouraging and endorsing the white collar criminals either through graft or absolute negligence or even indifference have uprooted the notion of governance and formed the basis on which modern-day corporate governance stands. Mindless abetment of bad practices by the government and its machinery has debunked our failure to embrace good corporate governance practices prior to liberalization.

An interesting study made by four business journalists in 2002 reveals how big business has been bleeding the banks for decades, yet it was kept under covers till the NPA bubble burst in the early 1990s. Tables 11.7 and 11.8 throw light on the groups involved in siphoning off banks' money and the default amount involved in such an act.

Table 11.7 *Debt Defaulters*

Company/Group	*Total Default (in Rs.Crore)*	*Company/Group*	*Total Default (in Rs.Crore)*
Mardia	1450	Lloyds	1012
Modern	846	Parasrampuria	705
Core Healthcare	751	Mafatlal	598
Nova	527.5	Patheja	547
Usha Ispat	391.7	Indian Charge Chrome Ltd	493.3
Altos India	437	JK	698
Rajinder	620	MESCO	527.5
Prakash Industries Ltd	360	Notes: (i) Information validated and dated to March 31, 2002; (ii) Defaults mean debt converted to NPAs and such NPAs recorded by banks and financial institutions.	

Source: Adapted from Halamkar S. et al (2002), "Rs.11,00,00,00,00,000: The Great Indian Robbery". Available on www.rediff.com

Table 11.8 *Declared Defaults*

Company/Group	*Total Default (in Rs.Crore)*	*Company/Group*	*Total Default (in Rs.Crore)*
Essar	7184	Malvika Steel	2095
Jindal Vijaynagar Steel	4900	SPIC	3284
Sanghi	1582	CESC Ltd	3300
IG Petrochemicals Ltd	720	Ispat Industries Ltd	6369
Ispat Metallics Ltd	1688	Notes: (i) Information validated and dated to March 31, 2002; (ii) Defaults mean declared defaults and that are likely to be harboring NPAs.	

Source: Adapted from Halamkar S. et al (2002), "Rs.11,00,00,00,00,000: The Great Indian Robbery". Available on www.rediff.com

But how did these defaults surface all of a sudden? In the previous section, you have seen how BIFR provided an easy exit to willful defaulters. While some companies have tried to go bankrupt to take shelter under SICA, some have still managed to willfully default without being referred to BIFR. Credit taken from a financial institution would often be diverted into unproductive activities by the promoter, and with the presence of a greedy and corrupt State machinery, default would often be used as a corporate strategy. Industrial licensing policies have been a bane of the nation and have helped in nurturing State-encouraged corporate mis-governance. Intense lobbying for licenses by capitalists and entrepreneurs meant a good opportunity for rent-seeking for the political class. Once licenses were granted, credit flowed into the entity without any questions being asked. Hence, one can argue that politicians had vested interests in directing institutional credit to their capitalistic cronies.[23]

Prior to banking reforms, public accountability and transparency were far-fetched ideas for the banking sector to comply with.[24] The reason for the surmounting NPAs was the bad quality of lending and collection by Indian banks. By "bad", I refer to the unprofessional excesses that the management of these banks committed under pressure from certain quarters of the State and its machinery, which finally led to recapitalization of banks at the expense of the public at large.[25] Politically driven credit knows no public accountability and obviously does not respect transparency to the least. Coupled with political intervention in credit direction, weak legal systems in the country have always shown us how myopic the government has been in framing its legal framework. To quote Chippalkatti N. and Rishi M.: "The market uncertainty generated by such deterioration in bank balance is only compounded by the weak regulatory environment in India and the moral hazard created by the government safety net". Whether such weaknesses were deliberately built in or were omitted due to oversight remain to be questioned. Poor laws reflect on the poor visionary balance of the State and its rather systemic weakness in pre-empting ex-post eventualities.

While legal recourse by banks to secure and execute collaterals of defaulting companies was pathetically awful, another important factor that spelt doom to the banking industry was the non-provisioning of information on borrowers' repayment records.[26] Under the secrecy clause of the country's banking laws, banks have always provided protection to the borrowers. This created a huge dent in the public exchequer, what with borrowers accessing loans from multiple banks. Banks too have been loath to provide credit history of the borrowers to other banks for fear of losing their clients. However, as one senior journalist contends, bankers and the employees' unions have often pressed the Reserve Bank of India and the Union Finance Ministry to reconsider the secrecy clause, for they felt that protection in the name of confidentiality gave a larger space for willful, large-scale defaulters an opportunity to escape public scrutiny.

While, on the one hand, bankers showed interest in greater transparency on defaulting accounts, on the other hand, "ever-greening" was extensively used as a default instrument by the lending banks as a cover-up to their collusive lending and collection practices.[27] A *Frontline* story of January 2000 states that there is a high-level of concentration in the top non-performing assets and the glory was cornered by the top industrial houses. It further states that just about 15 defaulters have accounted for about a third of the total NPAs of the Indian Bank, whereas in the Central Bank of India, the top 20 defaulters accounted for one-fifth of the bank's NPAs. This makes the argument of collusion between the banker and the industrialist more and more obvious.

A few cases of the banker-industrialist-politician nexus are listed below for the readers to gauge the amount of collusion that existed among this trio and which subsequently let down the country.

1. Kulwant Rai of the Usha group who had an ailing company in Malvika Steel was on IDBI's board for a long number of years, despite Malvika Steel's continued bleeding of IDBI's money.
2. Sanjay Lalbhai of the Arvind group who owed about Rs.2000 crores in debts and whose debts were subsequently restructured and pared down to Rs.1200 crores. Besides, ICICI acquired his dying company Anagram Finance despite knowing fully well that it was a dud company. Sanjay used to be a director on the ICICI board.

3. Jindal Group default of over Rs.6000 crores and yet the group had its representative on the IDBI board and also Jindal's graceful presence in the lower house as a member of the parliament.
4. Unit Trust of India's private placement in Reliance in 1994 to the tune of Rs.1073 crores, with a five year lock-in period. Subsequently, when the share prices abruptly fell from Rs.385 to Rs.77, the inability of UTI's fund managers in negotiating such a huge risk and their forays in buying out more and more shares to lower their average price of exposure.
5. Chairing of the CII's Task Force on Non-performing Assets in the Indian Financial System by K.V. Kamath, MD of ICICI. Ironically, it is the same CII whose members have been responsible for the huge exposures of ICICI to willful defaults.
6. Airports Authority of India doling out prime land and hangar space to the Mesco group at throwaway prices, at one-third the prevailing market prices, in 1992–93. This sale caused a loss of about Rs. 4 crore to the exchequer. All this happened despite Mesco Group's reputation in the market for financial embezzlements.

Remediation Efforts

Realization dawned on the State of its follies after India went begging in 1990 to the IMF for injecting funds into the economy for its survival.[28] With its recommendations to the Government of India for the near term, medium term and longer term, IMF has imposed on the country a strict condition which successive governments had to follow to the letter, to avoid the economic downfall of the country.

A few recommendations made by IMF to bring back Indian economy on the trail are listed below:

1. Reduce the budget deficit and start lowering the cash reserve and statutory liquidity requirements with the objective of

years and subsequently moving into market-determined interest rates on government debt.

2. Re-categorize immediately commercial bank lending to larger borrowers among small-scale industrialists and farmers, thus reducing the priority sector lending to about 20 percent. Reduce further the priority sector lending target to ten percent in three years.
3. Give commercial banks operational autonomy immediately and recapitalize them as needed after a portfolio clean-up. Introduce higher prudential norms, supervision standards and financial disclosure requirement. Improve legal procedures for foreclosure and sale or transfer of assets.
4. Allow competition by easing private sector entry and expansion.
5. Allow greater financial and operational autonomy to DFIs.
6. Allow private participation in the IDBI, IFCI and ICICI.
7. Privatize commercial banks, development banks and money capital markets.

Following IMF's directives, Narasimham Committee was constituted in 1991 to work out the first phase of banking reforms. The Committee in its report of 1992 suggested a move to a market-oriented banking system and strongly advocated the need "to operate in an environment of prudential regulation and transparent accounting". Another issue that made Indian banks quite unattractive was the fact that they could not meet the minimum capital adequacy as required by international norms set by the Basel committee. Except for the State Bank of India, no other Indian bank could manage the mandatory eight percent capital adequacy which could make it eligible to engage in forex trade. Sastry and Diwakar state that howsoever big and reputed the bank might be in India, if it did not meet the predetermined international norms, it was considered an outcast by the international banking community.

International pressure coupled with domestic failures compelled the government to react sharply to the mounting dissidence amongst the stakeholders. In an attempt to impose the "market disciplining" mechanism on the weak banks, the government had to divest its shareholding to the public, under duress.

In what is known as the first phase of banking reforms in India during the period 1992–98, the government had to finally admit that its ownership of public sector banks and institutions which held about 80% of market lending, and its failure to govern them, had led to its shocking exposure to the excesses of the industry. What remains to be questioned here is its belated realization of the fact that it was fostering corporate mis-governance all the while, from the time of Independence, in the name of development and for which the public had to pay the price twice—the first time when NPAs were declared and the second time when the government once again shamelessly robbed the exchequer in excess of Rs.20,000 crore towards recapitalizing the weak banks.

While in the first phase of reforms the government had agreed to bring down its ownership to 51%, subsequent to Narsimham Committee's second report on post-reforms developments, it had agreed to further prune its ownership down to 33% following the committee's recommendations. Also the government had gained wisdom, by refusing to recapitalize weak banks and asking them to raise money from the capital markets on the strength of their efficiency. The banks too are now doing their bit in improving disclosures which meet RBI regulatory requirements. Both the government and the banks have understood the need to adopt stricter lending practices, and income recognition and asset provisioning are supposedly being taken more seriously.

Narsimham II report has commented on the issue of "behest lending" and the role played by the government board nominees—usually politicians or industrial cronies of the State—in the operational issues of banks. Behest lending has been a responsible factor for poor asset quality and subsequently, providing a greater degree of protection to the borrowers.[29]

To control such protection to the borrowers and to seal all exit routes like the BIFR and multi-bank credit facilities, the Securitisation and Reconstruction of Financial Assets and Enforcement of Security Interest Bill (popularly known as the Securitisation Act) was passed in 2002 in the Parliament. This bill empowered the lenders to take possession of the collateral and recover their dues without waging a long battle in the court of law. The Securitisation Act dealt a big blow to the willful defaulters at large for its two-pronged provisions: a) if 75% or more of the secured creditors agree to recover their dues by executing their collateral, they can do so after serving a 60-day notice, and, b) the borrowers would be allowed to deflect this move by the secured creditors only if they deposit 75% of the total claimed amount in the Debt Recovery Tribunal where they could file an appeal.

The provisions in the Securitisation Act thus stand as big deterrents to willful defaulters. Thus it took about five decades for the government to recast its bank-debt recovery policies. Markets have been levelers the world over and in India it could be no different. Government that has willfully nurtured these willful defaulters had to succumb to international pressure in the post-liberalization period. Government indifference to the financial malaise in the country, as well as its breeding of corporate mis-governance in both the public and private sector have brought shame and deprecation for the country in the international community during the early period of liberalization. The bubble of corporate mis-governance had to finally burst and so did it in the face of liberalization.

In Conclusion

Government-industry nexus crippled the country of its competitiveness. Before the onset of liberalization, consumers were forced to accept whatever was on offer. Choice and variety that are so much an integral part of modern economies was a distant dream for the consumers in the pre-liberalization era.

From the above discussion, it becomes obvious that had the government been more responsible and had it played its fiduciary role properly, the latter day corporate governance problems could have been thwarted to some extent at least. While the government's legislations are an offshoot of "public interest", they have been comfortably captured by those parties that were presumably to be affected by these legislations. Public interest legislations are made with the understanding that markets are either ineffective in controlling inequities or have not matured enough to play a monitoring role and hence the government needs to frame legislation to curb expropriation of minority shareholders' wealth by the majority shareholder. While pre-nationalization banking industry was concentrated in the hands of a few industrialists and maharajas and credit rationing was supposedly done at the behest of the banker (who also held interests in other companies), priority sector never got the monies that it needed to grow. Through nationalization of banks, the government has indicated the import of national development via priority sector credit lending provisions. However, as mentioned earlier, despite nationalization, priority sector lending got stymied at just about 14% even as late as 1999. This fairly establishes the fact that industry has been a big beneficiary of credit allocations. If BIFR–SICA provisions and the net accumulated loss of all referred companies were any indication, if the massive non-performing assets in the banking system and systemic failures in executing collaterals were any indication, it can be fairly understood on how the regulatees ended up bending the regulations to their interests and captured them to their benefit.

While there are no quick-fixes to end industry-State nexus, the State should sincerely attempt to restrain the State-controlled institutions from committing to behest actions. Liberalisation and subsequent entry of multiple types of financial intermediaries has to some extent mitigated collusive practices. Financial investors have now become more responsible and are demanding transparent governance practices from companies, failing which they are unwilling to place equity or infuse debt capital in such companies. Government-owned financial companies should define the purpose of their business in clearer terms and endeavor to work for those objectives.[30]

Political intervention in the functioning of regulatory bodies should be completely done away with, and regulators need to be given the autonomy and powers to take decisions without being overawed by their political masters. Similarly, legal lead times need to be drastically shortened leaving no space for industry-State collusion.

DISCUSSION QUESTIONS

1. Refer to LIC-Mundhra scam in the chapter. Can you think of other recent examples of such scams? Look up the internet for information on Satyam scam.
2. Discuss the reforms undertaken in the banking sector in the post liberalization period.
3. "BIFR-SICA has been employed as an escape route by most defaulters". How true is this statement?

NOTES

1. Much alike the SEC of US, SEBI in India is empowered to regulate capital markets. It was established in 1992 and corporate governance norms were issued by it in 1998. Unlike the SEC, it is yet to get the much needed teeth to bite. Of late, it has been empowered with search and seizure rights and one can only expect it to dig its nails into scams more deeply.
2. Readers may find the data too dated. Throughout the chapter, only such data has been used that could help building up arguments for corporate mis-governance. Not that the current data inspires but that it fails to explain the context of corporate mis-governance properly.

3. For convenience, I have considered Insurance industry in conjunction with banking industry for the purpose of explanation of our viewpoint. It may, however, be noted that these two industries are widely different and the way they are governed is also different.
4. The six companies were: Richardson Cruddas, Jessops, Smith Stanistreet, Osler Lamps, Agnelo Brothers and British India Corporation. Of these six companies, except for the first two, the rest were all huge failures.
5. Since markets were punishing Mundhra's stocks and since it was felt that the retail shareholder was losing out due to this drag, LIC had to jump in with stock buys to avoid a collapse of Mundhra's stocks in the market.
6. Cases prior to that of Mundhra's are not known, nor is any evidence for any scam available prior to 1957. Hence we assume that the first seeds of corporate misgovernance were sown during the 1957 debacle and it took independent India as long as four decades after this, to come out with a code on corporate governance.
7. Verma, J.C. (1971), *Nationalization of Banks in India: a Detailed Analysis of Schemes and Proposals*, Career Digest Publications, New Delhi, for a detailed story.
8. In 1966, the minister mentioned this figure while delivering the Convocation address to the students of the University of Saugur.
9. See Bharat Jyoti, 22 September 1963.
10. State Banks of Travancore, Jaipur, Indore, Patiala, Saurashtra, Bikaner, Baroda, Mysore, Hyderabad, and smaller banks like that of Sangli, Manipur and Mayurbhanj.
11. Arvind (2001), Banking in India takes a Full Circle, Peoplesmarch, Vol. 2. No. 2, February.
12. Refer to Chapter IV of The Banking Companies (Acquisition and Transfer of Undertaking) Act, 1969. For example Section 10 (3) states: The Chairman of the existing bank holding office as such immediately before the commencement of this Act, shall be the Custodian of the corresponding new bank and shall receive the same emoluments as he was receiving immediately before such commencement: Provided that the Central government may, if the Chairman of an existing bank declines to become, or to continue to function as a Custodian of the corresponding new bank , or, if it is of opinion that it is necessary so to do, appoint any other person as the Custodian of a corresponding new bank and the Custodian so appointed shall receive such emoluments as the Central government may specify in this behalf.

13. Janardhan Poojary's bravado is an oft-repeated example to explain the loan mela phenomenon. In 1975, just before elections, Poojary organized loan melas in his constituency in Mangalore and got loans sanctioned to all the villagers who had applied for it. Once elections were won, he ensured that the loans were waived off by the banks. So much so for political interference. So much so for interfering with the governance of banks. The government and its organs must be held responsible for diluting the governance practices of corporations that led to a massive economic shock to the country in the early 1990s.
14. By government we mean all financial institutions controlled by the government like the DFI's, UTI, nationalized insurance companies and government-owned mutual funds.
15. "Different Strokes", in The Indian Express, 6 August 2001.
16. "In one of his many exit interviews ex-SEBI chairman D.R.Mehta expressed grave disquiet over the fact that 'corporations have become very powerful …' They are powerful in terms of their sheer size. The moment you start taking some action, they jump on you.' The influence of corporate houses is apparent in the investigations of the multi-party JPC which while aggressive with regulators, bankers and brokers, refused to examine industrialists despite three SEBI reports on the involvement of at least a dozen corporate houses in price manipulation with Ketan Parekh." (Kapur, D. and R. Ramamurthi, 2002)
17. Refer to Sick Industrial Companies (Special Provisions) Act, 1985.
18. "Between January 1997 and March 1998, the mean delay for the cases that were sanctioned restructuring schemes was almost double at 1664 days; while those that were recommended liquidation took 1468 days." (Goswami, 2000)
19. The very purpose for which SICA–BIFR was enacted stands defeated today. Tiwari Commission recommended its enactment to avoid a heavy drain on the exchequer that the sick industries caused. But this very provision provided an alibi to the industry to willfully siphon off money from the lending institution by deliberately taking the company into red.
20. One major criterion to determine sickness in an industrial company is that the accumulated losses of the company be equal to or more than its net worth i.e., its paid-up capital plus its free reserves.
21. An amendment in SICA in 1992 allowed PSUs to be referred to the BIFR. Till then, only the private sector companies were allowed to make use of SICA's provisions.

22. DFID Enterprise Development Strategy, London, Enterprise Development Division, Department for International Development.
23. Tarapore (2000) maintains: "In the public sector financial system management vests with the government and the top officials are merely the managers acting at the beckoning of the government."
24. Not that they are any good now, but with the adoption of Basel Committee report and following Narasimham I and Narsimham II reports, things seem to be a shade better.
25. A quote from Shri Krishnamurthy, Chairman, SBI from the Indian Banks' Survey, *Financial Express*, December 2001, would simplify this contention: "Who created this operating environment? First you, had loan melas, then waivers. Then we were chased to our non-performing assets. You ask banks to be all things to all people and then you see that there are NPAs and that recapitalization is bad. Let me tell you recapitalization is a price that we have to pay for what we did all along."
26. RBI studied about 10,000 large non-performing loans in 15 public sector banks and found difficulty involved even in obtaining judgment to execute the collateral and furthermore, still again difficulty in actually executing the collateral. Of the 10,000 cases that have been studied, amazingly, it was found that only one case had successfully executed the collateral after obtaining judgment. To top it all, judgment for such execution may come after a prolonged period of legal wrangles, usually about ten years. See Reserve Bank of India (1999), "Some Aspects and Issues Relating to NPAs in Commercial Banks," Department of Banking Supervision, *Reserve Bank of India Bulletin*, vol. LII, No. 7, pp. 913–36, RBI, Mumbai.
27. 'Ever-greening' refers to the pumping of more money to the debt defaulters with a view to : (a) paying up for their past debts; (b) using the newly acquired credit to revamp the firm for possible profits. In reality, this was just a make-up attempt by banks to hide their debts.
28. To quote Naik (2002), "Evidently, there seems to be a belated realization that the Indian financial sector is heading towards a major crisis because of the mounting bad loans and the inability of the lenders to recover them under the existing legal framework."
29. Readers are requested to go through Narsimham I and Narsimham II reports (Reports of the Committee on Banking Sector Reforms, 1992 and 1998) for a greater understanding of the reform initiatives undertaken by the government. The idea is to draw the readers' attention to the fact that corporate mis-governance has been constantly nurtured by the government till it received external shocks in the late

1980s and early 1990s and that the hue and cry on corporate governance is not just an overnight phenomenon. Though it existed even earlier, the government was abetting it in some form or the other, while post-liberalization, with the market playing a major role in the country's economy, market disciplining took a dominant form in shaping up corporate governance practices in the country. For the purpose of justifying my stand, I have looked at the investment/banking industry in the country and by no means is the study exhaustive in terms of explaining the functioning of the industry. I have only attempted to look at the industry and the role of the government from the corporate governance 'prism.'

30. For example, government-held insurance companies and mutual funds should be more focused on taking their small savers' savings on the growth track, rather than be a piggy-bank for the government's financial excesses. Readers may read this in line with the Haridhas Mundhra case mentioned in this chapter.

References and Bibliography

1. Ahmadjian, C.L., (2001), "Changing Japanese Corporate Governance", Working Paper No. 118, Columbia Business School.
2. Alchian A. and H. Demsetz, (1972), "Production, Information Costs, and Economic Organization", *The American Economic Review*, Vol. 62, pp. 777–95.
3. Anstey, V., (1929), *The Economic Development of India*, Longmans, Green and Company, London.
4. Arrow, K.J., (1974), *The Limits of Organization*, W.W. Norton, New York.
5. Arvind, (2001), "Banking in India takes a Full Circle", *Peoplesmarch*, Vol. 2, No. 2 February.
6. Asby, S., Swee Hoon, C. and Robert Hoffman, (2004), "Industry Self-Regulation: A Game-Theoretic Typology of Strategic Voluntary Compliance", *International Journal of the Economics of Business*, Vol. 11, pp. 91–106.
7. Baggot, R., (1989), "Regulatory Reform in Britain: The Changing Face of Self-Regulation", *Public Administration*, Vol. 67, pp. 435–54.
8. Bainbridge, M.S., (1995), "The Politics of Corporate Governance: Roe's Strong Managers, Weak Owners", Research Paper No. 01–10, *Research Paper Series*, UCLA School of Law, Los Angeles.

9. Bardhan, P., (1984), *The Political Economy of Development in India*, Oxford University Press, Oxford.
10. ———— (2003), "Political-Economy and Governance Issues in the Indian Economic Reform Process", K.R. Narayanan Oration, The Australia South Asia Research Centre, The Australian National University, Melbourne, 25 March 2003.
11. Barzel, Y., (1997), *Economic Analysis of Property Rights*, Second edition, Cambridge University Press, UK.
12. Beauchamp, L.T. and E.N. Bowie, (1997), *Ethical theory and Business*, Prentice-Hall, New Jersey.
13. Bebchuk, L.A. and M.J. Roe, (1999), "A Theory of Path Dependence in Corporate Governance and Ownership", Working Paper No. 131, Columbia Law School, The Center for Law and Economic Studies.
14. Becker, G.S., (1968), "Crime and Punishment: An Economic Approach", *Journal of Political Economy*, Vol. 76, pp. 169–217.
15. Belev, B., (2003), "Institutional Investors in Bulgarian Corporate Governance Reform: Obstacles or Facilitators?", *Journal of World Business*, Vol. 38, pp. 361–74.
16. Berglof, E. and E.V. Thadden, (1999), "The Changing Corporate Governance Paradigm: Implications for Transition and Developing Countries", William Davidson Institute Working Paper Series No. 263.
17. Berle, Adolf A. and M.C. Gardiner, (1932), *The Modern Corporation and Private Property*, Macmillan Publishing Company, New York.
18. Bevan, A.A., S. Estrin, and M.E. Schaffer, (1999), "Determinants of Enterprise Performance During Transition", CERT Discussion Paper No. 99/03.
19. Bhide, A., (1994), "Efficient Markets, Deficient Governance", *Harvard Business Review*, November–December, pp. 129–139.
20. Blair, M.M., (1995), Ownership and Control: Rethinking Corporate Governance for the Twenty-first Century, Brookings Institution, Washington DC.

21. Blasi, J. and A. Shleifer, (1996), "Corporate Governance in Russia: An Initial Look" in Frydman R., C.W. Gray, and A. Rapaczynski, edited *Corporate Governance in Central Europe and Russia*, Vol. 2: Insiders and the State, Budapest, pp. 78 –108.
22. Bolton, P. and E. Von Thadden, (1998), "Blocks, Liquidity and Corporate Control", *The Journal of Finance*, Vol. 53, pp. 1–25.
23. Bousmosieh, A.S. and D. M. Reeb, (2009), "Inside Directors, Managerial Competition and the Asymmetric Information Problem", Working Paper Series. Available on http://papers.ssrn.com/sol3/papers.cfm?abstract_id=674082
24. Braendle, U.C., A.N. Kostyuk, and R. Apreda, (2007), *Corporate Governance*, Virtus Interpress, Ukraine.
25. Briston, R.J. and R. Dobbins, (1978), "The Growth and Impact of Institutional Investors", A Report to the Research Committee of the Institute of Chartered Accountants in England and Wales, ICAEA, London.
26. Buono, A.F. and L.T. Nichols, (1989), *Stockholder and Stakeholder Interpretations of Business's Social Role* in *Business Ethics* edited by Hoffman M.W. and J.M. Moore, McGraw-Hill, New York.
27. Campbell, K., (2002), "Ownership Structure and the Operating Performance of Hungarian Firms", Working Paper No. 9, Centre for the Study of Economic and Social Change in Europe, London.
28. Carroll, A.B., (1997), "Three Dimensional Conceptual Model of Corporate Social Performance", *Academy of Management Review*, Vol. 4. pp. 497–506.
29. Chakroborty, S.K., (2000), "Corporate Governance for India—Some Pointers", *Productivity*, Vol. 40, No. 4, pp. 507–10.
30. Chandra, P., (1999), "Corporate Governance", in Kumar, T.R. edited Research Papers in Applied Finance, *The Applied Journal of Finance*, 1–7.

31. Charkham, J., (1994), *Keeping Good Company: A Study of Corporate Governance in Five Countries*, Clarendon Press, Oxford.
32. Charreaux and Desbrieres, (2001), "Corporate Governance: Stakeholder Value versus Shareholder Value", Research Paper, Unversite de Bourgogne, France. This paper was originally published in French in *Finance Controle Strategie*, Vol. 1, pp. 57–88.
33. Chew, D.H., (1997), *Studies in Corporate Finance and Governance Systems: A Comparison of the U.S., Japan and Europe*, Oxford University Press.
34. Chippalkatti N. and M. Rishi, (2003), "Indian Banking Sector Reform and Liberalization: Pain or Panacea?" Paper presented at the Academy of Business and Administrative Sciences International Conference held at Vancouver, Canada during June 24–26.
35. Cho, Y.J. and J.K. Kim, (1995), "Credit Policies and the Industrialisation of Korea", World Bank Discussion Paper No. 286, World Bank.
36. Claessens, S., S. Djankov, and G. Pohl, (1996), "Ownership and Corporate Governance: Evidence from Czech Republic", paper presented at the International Symposium on Capital Markets and Enterprise Reform in Beijing during November 8–9.
37. Coase, R.H., (1937), *The Nature of the Firm, Readings in Price Theory*, Homewood, II, Irwin, New Series, V: pp. 331–51.
38. Cochran, Philip L. and Steven I. Warwick, (1988), "Corporate Governance: A Review of Literature", Financial Executives Research Foundation, New Jersey.
39. Coffee Jr., J.C., (1999), "The Future as History: The Prospects for Global Convergence in Corporate Governance and its Implications", Working Paper No. 144, The Center for Law and Economic Studies, Columbia University School of Law.

40. Coffee Jr., J.C., (2000), "Convergence and its Critics: What Are The Preconditions to the Separation of Ownership and Control?" Working Paper No. 179. Columbia Law School, The Center for Law and Economic Studies, New York.
41. Cohen, S.S. and G. Boyd, (2000), *Corporate Governance and Globalization: Long Range Planning Issues*, Edward Elgar, UK.
42. Cowton, C. and R. Crisp, (1998), *Business Ethics: Perspectives on the Practice of Theory*, Oxford University Press, Oxford.
43. Crama, Y., L. Leruth, L. Renneboog, and J.P. Urbain, (1997), "Corporate Governance Structures, Control and Performance in European Markets: A Tale of Two Systems", Working Paper, Centre for Economic Research, Tilburg.
44. Dalal, (2000), "Bank Supervision and Accountability", available online at http://www.rediff.com/money/2000/mar/28dalal.htm
45. Dalton, D.R. and I.F. Kesner, (1985), "Organizational Performance as an Antecedent of Inside/Outside Chief Executive Succession: An Empirical Assessment", *Academy of Management Journal*, Vol. 28. pp. 749–62.
46. David, P.A., (1985), "Clio and the economics of QWERTY", *American Economic Review*, Vol. 2, No. 75, pp. 332–37.
47. ———— (1994), "Why are Institutions the Carriers of History? Path Dependence and the Evolution of Conventions, Organizations and Institutions", *Structural Change and Economic Dynamics*, Vol. 5, No. 2, pp. 205–20.
48. Davies, A., (1999), *A Strategic Approach to Corporate Governance*, Gower, Hampshire.
49. Davis, E.P., (1995), *Pension Funds, Retirement-Income Security and Capital Markets: An International Perspective*, Oxford University Press, Oxford.
50. ———— and B. Steill, (2001), *Institutional Investors*, The MIT Press, Cambridge, MA.

51. Dehaene A., V. De Vuyst, and Ooghe Hubert, (2001), "Corporate Performance and Board Structure in Belgian Companies", *Long Range Planning*, Vol. 34, pp. 383–98.
52. Demsetz, H., (1983), "The Structure of Ownership and the Theory of the Firm", *Journal of Law and Economics*, Vol. 26, pp. 375–90.
53. ———— and K. Lehn, (1985), "The Structure of Corporate Ownership: Causes and Consequences", *Journal of Political Economy*, Vol. 93, pp. 1155–77.
54. Denis, D. and D. Denis, (1994), "Majority Owner-Managers and Organizational Efficiency", *Journal of Corporate Finance*, Vol. 1, pp. 91–118.
55. Denis, D.K., (2001), "Twenty-five Years of Corporate Governance Research ... and Counting", *Review of Financial Economics*, Vol. 10, pp. 191–212.
56. Denis, D.J., D.K. Denis, and A. Sarin, (1997), "Agency Problems, Equity Ownership and Corporate Diversification", *Journal of Finance*, Vol. 52, pp. 135–60.
57. Denis, K. Diane and J. John McConnell, (2003), "International Corporate Governance", *Journal of Financial and Quantitative Analysis*, Vol. 38, No. 1 pp. 1–36.
58. DesJardins, R.J. and J.J. McCall, (2000), *Contemporary Issues in Business Ethics*, Wadsworth, Belmont.
59. DFID, (2000), DFID Enterprise Development Strategy, London, Enterprise Development Division, Department for International Development.
60. Dienhart, W.J., (2000), *Business, Institutions and Ethics: A Text with Cases and Readings*, Oxford University Press, New York.
61. Djankov, S., (1999), "Ownership Structure and Enterprise Restructuring in Six Newly Independent States", Working Paper Series No. 2047, World Bank.
62. Donaldson, T. and P.H. Werhane, (1979), *Ethical Issues in Business: A Philosophical Approach*, Prentice-Hall Inc, New Jersey.

63. Drutman, L., (2002), "The History of the Corporation", Citizen Works Corporate Power Discussion Groups, Session II, Reading I. Available at http://www.citizenworks.org/corp/dg/s2r1.pdf.
64. Dutta, S., (1997), *Family Business in India*, Response Books, New Delhi.
65. Eisenberg, M.A., (1976), *The Structure of the Corporation: A Legal Analysis*, Beard Books, Maryland.
66. ——— (1993), *The Business Lawyer*, Vol. 48, No. 4, p. 1275.
67. ——— (1999), "The Conception that the Corporation is a Nexus of Contracts and the Dual Nature of Firms", *Journal of Corporation Law*, Vol. 24, pp. 819.
68. Estrin, S., J. Konings, Z. Zolkiewski and M. Angelucci, (2001), "The Effect of Ownership and Competitive Pressures on Firm Performance in Transition Countries: Micro-evidence from Bulgaria, Romania and Poland", Working Paper, Licos Centre for Transition Economics.
69. Fama, E.F., (1980), "Agency Problems and the Theory of the Firm", *Journal of Political Economy*, Vol. 88, pp. 288–307.
70. Fama, E.F., and M.C. Jensen, (1983), "Separation of Ownership and Control", *Journal of Law and Economics*, Vol. 26, pp. 301–25.
71. Foss, N.J., (1997), "On the Relations between Evolutionary and Contractual Theories of the Firm", Working Paper No. 97–4, Department of Industrial Economics and Strategy, Copenhagen Business School, Denmark.
72. ——— (1998), "The Theory of the Firm: An Introduction to Themes and Contributions", published in Foss, N.J. edited *Theories of the firm: Critical Perspectives in Economic Organization* (3 vols.), London, Routledge.
73. Friedman, M., (1997), "The Social Responsibility of Business is to Increase Profits" in Beauchamp, L.T. and E.N. Bowie edited *Ethical Theory and Business*, Prentice-Hall, New Jersey, pp. 56–61.

74. Frydman, R., C. Gray, M. Hessel, and A. Rapaczynski, (1997), "Private Ownership and Corporate Performance: Some Lessons from Transition Economies", Working Paper, C.V.Starr Center, New York University.

75. ——— (1998), "Why Ownership Matters? Entrepreneurship and the Restructuring of Enterprises in Central Europe", Working Paper No. 172, Columbia Law School, The Center for Law and Economic Studies, New York.

76. Gedajlovic, E.R., T. Yoshikawa, and M. Hashimoto, (2001), "Ownership Structure, Investment Behavior and Firm Performance in Japanese Manufacturing Industries", Discussion Paper, Erasmus Research Institute of Management, Erasmus University, Rotterdam.

77. Gerlach, M.L., (1992), *Alliance Capitalism: The Social Organisation of Japanese Business*, Berkeley, University of California Press.

78. Ghosh, T.P., (2000), "Corporate Governance Models and Disclosures", *Productivity*, Vol. 40, No. 4, pp. 519–29.

79. Gill, A., (2008), "Corporate Governance as Social Responsibility", *Berkeley Journal of International Law*, Vol. 26, No. 2, pp. 452–78.

80. Godbole, M., (2002), "Corporate Governance: Myth and Reality", *Economic and Political Weekly*, Vol. 37, No. 30, pp. 3094–3102.

81. Goldstone, J.A., (1998), "Initial Conditions, General Laws, Path Dependence and Explanation in Historical Sociology", *American Journal of Sociology*, Vol. 104, No. 3, pp. 829–45.

82. Gorringe, P.A., (1995), "Path Dependence—Causes, Consequences and Policy", First Draft, Discussion Paper, The Treasury Wellington, New Zealand.

83. Goswami, O., (2000), "The Tide Rises, Gradually: Corporate Governance in India", Draft, Presented at the Informal Workshop on Corporate Governance in Developing Countries and Emerging Economies, 3–4 April 2000, Paris.

84. Government of India, (1963), Report of Justice Vivian Bose Commission, New Delhi.
85. Government of India, (1956), The Companies Act, New Delhi: Ministry of Law, Department of Justice and Company Affairs.
86. Government of India, (1969), Report of the Industrial Licensing Policy Inquiry Committee, New Delhi.
87. Grossman, S. and O. Hart, (1983), "An Analysis of the Principal-Agent Problem", *Econometrica*, Vol. 51, pp. 7–45.
88. ——— (1986), "The Costs and Benefits of Ownership: A Theory of Vertical and Lateral Integration", *Journal of Political Economy*, Vol. 94, pp. 691–719.
89. Guillen, M., (1999), "Corporate Governance and Globalization: Arguments and Evidence against Convergence", Working Paper, Reginald H. Jones Center.
90. Gupta, A.K. and L.J. Lad, (1983), "Industry Self-Regulation: An Economic, Organizational and Political Analysis", *Academy of Management Review,* Vol. 8, No. 3, pp. 416–25.
91. Halamkar S. et al., (2002), "Rs.11,00,00,00,00,000: The Great Indian Robbery". Available on www.rediff.com.
92. Hanson, J.A., (2001), "Indian Banking: Market Liberalization and the Pressures for Institutional and Market Framework Reform", Working Paper No. 104, Center for Research and Economic Development and Policy Research, Stanford University, Stanford.
93. Harper, J.T., (2002), "The Performance of Privatized Firms in the Czech Republic", *Journal of Banking and Finance*, Vol. 26, pp. 621–49.
94. Hart, O., (1995), "Corporate Governance: Some Theoretical Implications", *The Economic Journal*, Vol. 105, pp. 678–89.
95. ——— J. Moore, (1999), "Foundations of Incomplete Contracts", *Review of Economic Studies*, Vol. 66, No. 1, pp. 115–38.

96. Hawley, P.J. and A.T. Williams, (2000), "The Rise of Fiduciary Capitalism: How Institutional Investors Can Make Corporate America More Democratic", University of Pennsylvania Press, Philadelphia.
97. Hedlund, S., (2000), "Path Dependence in Russian Policy Making: Constraints on Putin's Economic Choice", *Post-Communist Economies*, Vol. 12, No. 4, pp. 389–407.
98. Hilton Root, (1998), "India: Asia's Next Tiger?" Essay in Public Policy No. 82, Hoover Institution. Available online at http://www-hoover.stanford.edu/publications/epp/82/a.html.
99. Holderness, C.G., K. Randal, and S. Dennis, (1999), "Were the Good Old Days That Good? Changes in Managerial Stock Ownership Since the Great Depression", *Journal of Finance*, Vol. 54, No. 2, pp. 435–70.
100. ——— D.P. Sheehan, (1988), "The Role of Majority Shareholders in Publicly held Corporations: An Exploratory Analysis", *Journal of Financial Economics*, Vol. 20, pp. 317–46.
101. Hopt, K., H. Kanda, M.J. Roe, E. Wymersch, and S. Prigge, (1998), *Comparative Corporate Governance: The State of the Art of Emerging Research*, Clarendon Press, Oxford.
102. Howard R. Bowen, (1953), *Social Responsibilities of the Businessman*, Harper & Brothers, New York.
103. Jacoby, M.S., (2001), "Corporate Governance in Corporate Perspective: Prospects for Convergence", *Comparative Labor Law and Policy Journal*, Vol. 22, No. 1, pp. 5–32.
104. Jensen, M.C., (1986), "Agency Costs of Free Cash Flow, Corporate Finance and Takeovers", *American Economic Review*, Vol. 76, pp. 323–29.
105. ——— (1993), "The Modern Industrial Revolution, Exit and the Failure of Internal Control Systems", *Journal of Finance*, Vol. 48, pp. 831–80.

106. Jensen, M.C. and W.H. Meckling, (1976), "Theory of the Firm: Managerial Behavior, Agency Costs and Ownership Structure", *Journal of Financial Economics*, Vol. 4, pp. 305–360.

107. ———— W.H. Meckling, (2006), "Corporate Governance and 'Economic Democracy': An Attack on Freedom", Proceedings of Corporate Governance: A Definitive Exploration of the Issues", C.J. Huizenga (ed) UCLA Extension, 1983. Available at SSRN: http://ssrn.com/abstract=321521.

108. ———— R. Ruback, (1983), "The Market for Corporate Control: The Scientific Evidence", *Journal of Financial Economics*, Vol. 11, pp. 5–50.

109. ———— J. B. Warnet, (1988), "The Distribution of Power Among Corporate Managers, Shareholders and Directors", *Journal of Financial Economics*, Vol. 20, pp. 3–24.

110. Jones, J. and M. Pollitt, (1998), *The Role of Business Ethics in Economic Performance*, Macmillan Press Ltd: London.

111. Kaminski, B. and M. Ribound, (2000), "Foreign Investment and Restructuring: The Evidence from Hungary", World Bank Technical Paper No. 453, Washington: The World Bank.

112. Kane, E.J., (1981), "Impact of Regulation on Economic Behavior", *The Journal of Finance*, Vol. 36, pp. 355–67.

113. ———— (1983), "Policy Implications of Structural Changes in Financial Markets", *American Economic Review*, Vol. 73, pp. 96–100.

114. Kanfer, F.H. and P. Karoly, (1972), "Self-control: A Behavioristic Excursion Into the Lion's Den", Behavior Therapy, Vol. 3, pp. 398–416.

115. Kang, L.D. and B.A. Sorenson, (1999), "Ownership Organization and Firm Performance", *Annual Review of Sociology*, Vol. 25, pp. 121–44.

116. Kay and Vickers, (1988), "Regulatory Reform in Britain", *Economic Policy*, Vol. 5, pp. 286–351.

117. Keasey, K., S. Thompson, and M. Wright, (1997), *Corporate Governance: Economic, Management and Financial Issues*, Oxford University Press: Oxford.

118. Keasey, K. and M. Wright, (1997), *Corporate Governance: Responsibilities, Risks and Remuneration*, John Wiley and Sons Ltd: London.

119. Khanna, T. and K. Palepu, (1999), "Emerging Market Business Groups, Foreign Investors and Corporate Governance", Working Paper No. 6955, National Bureau of Economic Research.

120. ———— (2000), "Is Group Affiliation Profitable in Emerging Markets? An Analysis of Diversified Indian Business Groups", *The Journal of Finance*, Vol. 55, No. 2, pp. 867–91.

121. Kobrak, P., (2002), *Cozy Politics: Political Parties, Campaign Finance, and Compromised Governance*, Lynne Reinner Publishers: London.

122. Koehn, D., (1994), *The Ground of Professional Ethics*, Routledge: New York.

123. Kester, W.C., (1991), "Japanese Corporate Governance and the Conservation of Value in Financial Distress", *The Continental Bank Journal of Applied Corporate Finance*, Vol. 4, No. 2, pp. 98–104.

124. Kuchhal, S.C., (1960), *The Industrial Economy of India*, Chaitanya Publishing House, Allahabad, India, pp. 397.

125. Kuznetsov, P. and A. Muravyev, (2001), "Ownership Structure and Firm Performance in Russia: The Case of Blue Chips of the Stock Market", Working Paper, Russian-European Centre for Economic Policy.

126. Kyd, S., (1794), *Corporation*, Vol. 1, p. 13.

127. La Porta, R., F. Lopez-de-Silanes, and A. Shleifer, (1999), "Investor Protection and Corporate Governance", The National Bureau of Economic Research Working Paper, 7403.

128. La Porta, R., F. Lopez-de-Silanes, and A. Shleifer, (1999), "Corporate Ownership Around the World", *Journal of Finance*, Vol. 54, pp. 471–517.
129. La Porta, R., F. Lopez-de-Silanes, A. Shleifer, A, and R.W. Vishny, (1998), "Law and Finance", *Journal of Political Economy*, Vol. 106, pp. 1113–1155.
130. Lee, K., (1999), "Corporate Governance and Growth in the Korean Chaebols: A Microeconomic Foundation for the 1997 Crisis", Working Paper No.18, Institute of Economic Research, Seoul National University.
131. Lepley, R., (1949), *Value: A Cooperative Inquiry*, Columbia University Press: New York.
132. Margaret, J., (2001), "A History of Corporate Governance: The Case of Burns Philip & Company Limited, an Australian Perspective", Draft, Deakin University, Australia.
133. Mathiesen, H., (1999), *Managerial Ownership and Financial Performance*, Unpublished doctoral dissertation, Copenhagen Business School, Denmark. Available on http://www.e.viaminvest.com
134. McCarthy, D.J. and S.M. Puffer, (2003), "Corporate Governance in Russia: A Framework for Analysis", *Journal of World Business*, Vol. 38, No. 4, pp. 397–415.
135. McDaniel, T., (1996), *The Agony of the Russian Idea*, Princeton University Press.
136. McChesney, F., (1997), *Money for Nothing: Politicians, Rent Extraction and Political Extortion*, Harvard University Press: Cambridge.
137. McGregor, L., (2000), *The Human Face of Corporate Governance*, Palgrave, New Jersey.
138. McIntosh, M., D. Leipziger, K. Jones, and G. Coleman, (1998), *Corporate Citizenship: Successful strategies for Responsible Companies*, London, *Financial Times*, Pitman Publishing.

139. Mehran, H., (1995), "Executive Compensation Structure, Ownership and Firm Performance", *Journal of Financial Economics*, Vol. 38, pp. 163–84.
140. Mehta, M.M., (1952), *The Combination Movement in Indian Industries*, Friends' Book Depot: Allahabad.
141. Merchant, K.T., (1970), "Management Change in Companies", *Economic and Political Weekly*, Vol. 5, No. 23, pp. 921–23.
142. Minogue, M., (2002), Governance-based Analysis of Regulation, Centre on Regulation and Competition, Vol. 3, Working Paper Series, University of Manchester, UK.
143. Mintzberg, H., (1983), *Power In and Around Organizations*, Prentice-Hall.
144. Mishra, R.K. and B. Navin, (2000), Corporate Governance and Public Enterprise Boards", *Productivity*, Vol. 40, No. 4, January–March, pp. 544–549.
145. Mohanty, P., (2002), "Institutional Investors and Corporate Governance in India", NSE Research Paper No. 15, National Stock Exchange, India.
146. Monks, R. and N. Minow, (1995), *Corporate Governance*, Blackwell Publishers: New York.
147. Mookherjee, D., (1999), Contractual Constraints on Firm Performance in Developing Countries, Mimeo Department of Economics, Boston University.
148. Morck, R., A. Shleifer, and R.W. Vishny, (1988), "Management ownership and market valuation: an empirical analysis", *Journal of Financial Economics*, Vol. 20, pp. 292–315.
149. Mukherjee Reed, A., (2001), *Perspectives on the Indian Corporate Economy: Exploring the Paradox of Profits*, Palgrave: New York.
150. Murthy, K.R.S., (1998), "Corporate Governance: A Sociological Perspective", *ASCI Journal of Management*, Vol. 27.
151. Naik, S.D., (2002), NPA "Ordinance-Empowering the Financial Sector", available online at http://www.thehindubusinessline.com/bline/2002/08/07/stories/2002080700050800.htm.

152. Naughton, T., (2002), "Corporate Governance: An International Perspective", Professional Lecture Series Monograph, Griffith University, Brisbane.

153. North, D., (1990), *Institutions, Institutional Change and Economic Performance*, Cambridge University Press: Cambridge.

154. Ogus, A.I., (1994), *Regulation: Legal Form and Economic Theory*, Oxford University Press.

155. Oman, C., (2001), "Corporate Governance and National Development", Technical Paper, Paper No. 180, OECD Development Centre.

156. O'Sullivan, A.M., (2000), *Contests for Corporate Control: Corporate Governance and Economic Performance in the United States and Germany*, Oxford University Press: New York, pp. 70–145.

157. Packer, F. and M. Ryser, (1992), "The Governance of Failure: An Anatomy of Corporate Bankruptcy in Japan", Working Paper No. 62, Center on Japanese Economy and Business, Columbia University.

158. Panchali, J. and N. Desai, (1999), "Ownership Structure and Financial Performance", in Ravi Kumar, T. edited "Research Papers in Applied Finance", *The ICFAI Journal of Applied Finance*, Hyderabad.

159. Parker, D., (1999), "Regulating Public Utilities: What Other Countries can Learn from the UK Experience", *Public Management*, Vol. 1, No. 1, pp. 93–120.

160. Patibandla, (2001), "Equity Pattern, Corporate Governance and Performance: A Study of India's Corporate Sector", Working Paper 9–2001, Copenhagen Business School, Copenhagen.

161. Peltzmann, S., (1976), "Toward a More General Theory of Regulation", *Journal of Law and Economics*, Vol. 19, pp. 211–40.

162. Pierson, P., (2000), "Increasing Returns, Path Dependence and the Study of Politics", *American Political Science Review*, Vol. 94, pp. 251–268.

163. Pinteris, G., (2002), "Ownership Structure, Board Characteristics and Performance of Argentine Banks", Incomplete Draft, University of Illinois.
164. Polinsky, A.M. and S. Shavell, (2000), "The Economic Theory of Public Enforcement of Law", *Journal of Economic Literature*, Vol. 38, pp. 45–76.
165. Porter, M.E., and M.R. Kramer, (2006), "Strategy and Society: The Link Between Competitive Advantage and Corporate Social Responsibility", Harvard Business Review, Vol. 84, No. 12, pp. 78–92.
166. Posner, R.A., (1974), "Theories of Economic Regulation", *The Bell Journal of Economics and Management Science*, Vol. 5, pp. 336.
167. Pound, J., (1995), "The Promise of the Governed Corporation", Harvard Business Review, Vol. 73, pp. 89–98.
168. Prowse S.D., (1992), "The Structure of Corporate Ownership in Japan", *Journal of Finance*, Vol. 47, pp. 1121–40.
169. Purcell, M., (2002), "The State, Regulation and Global Restructuring: Reasserting the Political in Political Economy", *Review of International Political Economy*, Vol. 9, No. 2, pp. 298–332.
170. Rado B., and S.M. Bainbridge, (2001), Corporate Governance in Post-Privatized Slovenia, Vol. 49, pp. 49.
171. Rajan, R. and L. Zingales, (1988), "The Governance of the New Enterprise", Working Paper, University of Chicago.
172. Reynolds, L., (1981), "Foundations of an Institutional Theory of Regulation", *Journal of Economic Issues*, Vol. 15, No. 3, pp. 641–56.
173. Roe, M.J., (1990), "Political and Legal Restraints on Ownership and Control of Public Companies", *Journal of Financial Economics*, Vol. 27, pp. 7–42.
174. ———— (1994), *Weak Owners, Strong Managers: The Political Roots of American Corporate Finance*, Princeton University Press, Princeton, NJ.

175. Roe, M.J., (1997), "Comparative Corporate Governance", *Palgrave Dictionary of Law and Economics*, Harvard Law School.

176. ———— (2000), "Political Foundations for Separating Ownership from Corporate Control", Working Paper No. 155, Columbia Law School, The Center for Law and Economic Studies, New York.

177. Ross, S.A., (1973), "The Economic Theory of Agency: The Principal's Problem", *American Economic Review*, Vol. 63, No. 2, pp. 134–39.

178. Rubach, M.J., and T.C. Sebora, (1998), "Comparative Corporate Governance: Competitive Implications of an Emerging Convergence", *Journal of World Business*, Vol. 33, No. 2, pp. 167–84.

179. Rungta, R.S., (1970), *The Rise of Business Corporations in India: 1851–1900*, Cambridge University Press: Cambridge.

180. Sastry and Diwakar, (2001), "More on Bank Privatisation, Liberation", available online at http://www.cpiml.org/liberation/year_2001/february/10_20labour.htm

181. Schmidt, R.H. and G. Spindler, (2002), "Path Dependence, Corporate Governance and Complementarity", *International Finance*, Vol. 5, No. 3, pp. 311–333.

182. Sengupta, N.K., (2001), *Government and Business*, Vikas Publishing House Pvt. Limited, New Delhi.

183. Sharma, T. and S.D. Chauhan, (1965), *Indian Industries*, Shiv Lal Agarwala & Co, Agra.

184. Sherman, H. and R. Chaganti, (1998), *Corporate Governance and Timeliness of Change: Reorientation in 100 American Firms*, Quorum: BooksWestport, CT.

185. Shleifer, A. and R.W. Vishny, (1986), "Large Shareholders and Corporate Control", *Journal of Political Economy*, Vol. 94, pp. 461–88.

186. ———— (1997), "A Survey of Corporate Governance", *Journal of Finance*, Vol. 52, pp. 737–83.

187. Short, H., (1994), "Ownership, Control, Financial Structure and the Performance of Firms", *Journal of Economic Surveys*, Vol. 8, No. 3, pp. 203–50.
188. ———— Short, H. and K. Keasey, (1999), "Managerial Ownership and the Performance of Firms: Evidence from the U.K.", *Journal of Corporate Finance*, Vol. 5, pp. 79–101.
189. Singer, P., (1991), *A companion to Ethics*, Blackwell Publishers, Masachusetts.
190. Smerdon, R., (1998), *A Practical Guide to Corporate Governance*, Sweet and Maxwell: London.
191. Spierings, R., (1990), "Reflections on the Regulation of Financial Intermediaries", *KYKLOS*, Vol. 43, pp. 91–109.
192. Sridhar, V., (2000), "A Controversial Report", *Frontline*, Vol. 17, No. 1, Jan. 8–21.
193. Sternberg, E., (1998), Corporate Governance: Accountability in the Marketplace, London: Institute of Economic Affairs.
194. Sakuma, K., (2001), "Japan: Country Report", in Gugler, K. edited *Corporate Governance and Economic Performance*, Oxford University Press, pp. 139–55.
195. Stigler, G.J., (1971), "The Theory of Economic Regulation", *Bell Journal of Economics and Management Sciences*, Vol. 2, pp. 3–21.
196. Stulz, R.M., (1988), "Managerial Control of Voting Rights: Financing Policies and the Market for Corporate Control", *Journal of Financial Economics*, Vol. 20, pp. 25–54.
197. Sutton, B., (1993), *The Legitimate Corporation: Essential Readings in Business Ethics and Corporate Governance*, Basil Blackwell Limited: London.
198. Thomsen, S. and T. Pedersen, (1997), "Industry and Ownership Structure, Institute of International Economics and Management", Copenhagen Business School, Working Paper 6–1997.
199. Tirole, J., (2001), "Corporate Governance", *Econometrica*, Vol. 69, No. 1, pp. 1–35.

200. Trevino, K.L., P. L. Hartman, and M. Brown, (2000), "Moral Person and Moral Manager: How Executives Develop a Reputation for Ethical Leadership", *California Management Review*, Vol. 42, No. 4, pp. 128–42.
201. Tsui, A.S. and S. J. Ashford, (1994), "Adaptive Self-regulation: A Process View of Managerial Effectiveness", *Journal of Management*, Vol. 20, No. 1, pp. 93–121.
202. Turnbull, S., (2000), "Corporate Governance: Theories, Challenges and Paradigms", *Journal of Economic Literature*, Vol. 1, No. 1, pp. 11–43.
203. Uche, U.C., (2001), "The Theory of Regulation: A Review Article", *Journal of Financial Regulation and Compliance*, Vol. 9, No. 1, pp. 67–80.
204. Velasquez, G.M., (1992), *Business Ethics: Concepts and Cases*, Prentice-Hall, New Jersey.
205. Verma, J.C., (1971), *Nationalization of Banks in India: A Detailed Analysis of Schemes and Proposals*, Career Digest Publications, New Delhi.
206. Vincensini, C., (2001), "Is Path Dependence a Useful Concept to Analyse the Evolution of Ownership Structures in Central Europe? A Theoretical and Empirical Discussion", Conference Paper, IMAD, Ototec, Slovenia, 13–14 July 2001.
207. Walsh, P.P. and C. Whelan, (2000), "Firm Performance and the Political Economy of Corporate Governance: Survey Evidence for Bulgaria, Hungary, Slovakia and Slovenia", Discussion Paper Number 85, Licos Centre for Transition Economies, Belgium.
208. Ware, R.F., (1975), "Performance of Manager-versus Owner-Controlled Firms in the Food and Beverage Industry", *Quarterly Review of Economics and Business*, Summer, 1975, Vol. 15, pp. 81–92.
209. Wei, Z., O. Varela, and K.M. Hassan, (2002), "Ownership and Performance in Chinese Manufacturing Industry", *Journal of Multinational Financial Management*, Vol. 12, pp. 61–78.

210. Weir, C. and D. Lang, (2001), "Governance Structures, Director Independence and Corporate Performance in the UK", *European Business Review*, Vol. 13, pp. 86–94.
211. Weisbach, M.S., (1988), "Outside Directors and CEO Turnover", *Journal of Financial Economics*, Vol. 20, pp. 431–60.
212. Werhane, P. and R. Freeman, (1999), "Business Ethics: The State-of-the-Art", *International Journal of Management Review*, Vol. 1, No. 1, pp.1–16.
213. Williamson, O.E., (1988), "Corporate Finance and Corporate Governance", *Journal of Finance*, Vol. 43, No. 3, pp. 567–91.
214. Xu, C. and K. Pistor, (2003), "Law Enforcement under Incomplete Law: Theory and Evidence from Financial Market Regulation", Working Paper No. 222, The Centre for Law and Economic Studies, Columbia Law School.
215. Xu, X. and Y. Wang, (1997), "Ownership Structure, Corporate Governance and Firm Performance: The Case of Chinese Stock Companies", Working Paper, World Bank.
216. Zingales, L., (1997), Corporate Governance in The New Palgrave Dictionary of Economics and Law, Macmillan: London.

INDEX

C

D

E

For Product Safety Concerns and Information please contact our EU representative GPSR@taylorandfrancis.com
Taylor & Francis Verlag GmbH, Kaufingerstraße 24, 80331 München, Germany

www.ingramcontent.com/pod-product-compliance
Ingram Content Group UK Ltd.
Pitfield, Milton Keynes, MK11 3LW, UK
UKHW022033061126
477531UK00008B/297
* 9 7 8 1 1 3 8 6 6 2 7 4 2 *